why preservation matters

yale

university

press

new haven

and

london

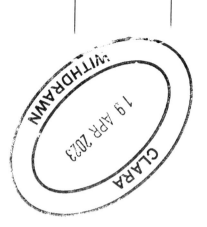

max

page

why

preservation

matters

Published with assistance from the Kingsley Trust
Association Publication Fund established by the
Scroll and Key Society of Yale College.

Yale University Press books may be purchased in
quantity for educational, business, or promotional use.
For information, please e-mail sales.press@yale.edu
(U.S. office) or sales@yaleup.co.uk (U.K. office).

Set in Times Roman and Adobe Garamond types by
Integrated Publishing Solutions.

Printed in the United States of America.

Library of Congress Control Number: 2016937786
ISBN 978-0-300-21858-9 (hardcover : alk. paper)

A catalogue record for this book is available from the
British Library.

This paper meets the requirements of ANSI/NISO
Z39.48-1992 (Permanence of Paper).

10 9 8 7 6 5 4 3 2 1

The Creative Destruction of Manhattan, 1900–1940

The City's End: Two Centuries of Fantasies, Fears, and Premonitions of New York's Destruction

Building the Nation: Americans Write About Their Architecture, Their Cities, and Their Environment (co-edited with Steven Conn)

Giving Preservation a History: Histories of Historic Preservation in the United States (co-edited with Randall Mason)

The Future of Higher Education (with Dan Clawson)

Reconsidering Jane Jacobs (co-edited with Tim Mennell)

Campus Guide to the University of Massachusetts (with Marla Miller)

Memories of Buenos Aires: Signs of State Terrorism in Argentina (editor)

Bending the Future: 50 Ideas for the Next 50 Years of Historic Preservation (co-edited with Marla Miller)

contents

As the fiftieth anniversary of the 1966 National Historic Preservation Act approaches, it seems like an appropriate time to make an assessment of the effect that preservation policy and action have had on life in the United States, while also offering proposals for how preservation can be an even greater progressive force in the years to come. I also look beyond the boundaries of the United States, to places of historic importance around the world and the ways people are working to save them and tell their stories. I believe that just as the American movement on which I focus in this book can have relevance for people doing the work of building a progressive preservation movement in other countries, their work can have relevance for the U.S. preservation movement—for the values that I shall argue need to be part of the preservation movement of the future are human, not national values.

I wrote much of this book while on sabbatical in Medellín, Colombia, a place in which debates around preservation and memory have been particularly vital in recent years. Although I touch only briefly on those debates in my prologue, that swirl of discussion inevitably became background to my writing.

This book is the product of two decades of thinking about historic preservation, and has been anchored in experiences made possible by generous people and institutions.

Time to think, time to visit places, time to write—these are the greatest gifts to a scholar and writer. The University of Massachusetts, Amherst, and the College of Humanities and Fine Arts have been enormously supportive of my research and writing over the fifteen years I have been at the university. Six months at the American Academy as a Rome Prize Fellow in 2014 was a life-changing gift, allowing me to think about historic preservation in the company of brilliant, creative scholars and designers in a city that is an outdoor exhibition of preservation philosophies and techniques.

The Howard Foundation and the Marion Jasper Whiting Foundation offered me the chance to venture far beyond the United States—to Argentina, Japan, Dubai, India, and China—to explore how preservationists in other places wrestle with the question of what from the past should be brought into the future. In 2009, I was given the opportunity by the Fulbright Foundation to live and teach in Buenos Aires, in the midst of Argentina's confrontation with its violent past.

I was thrilled that Steve Wasserman was so passionate about having me write this volume for Yale University Press; he helped shape my approach from the start. Susan Laity was the outstanding manuscript editor I had been hoping for. Where the sentences flow, and logic follows, you will experience her mark on the book. I am humbled to be a part of the Why X Matters series, which features some of my intellectual heroes. I owe a continuing debt to Georges Borchardt for guiding me from book proposals to publications over the past decade. Special thanks as well to my friends Tom Mayes and Richard Rabinowitz for not only inspiring the ideas in the book through years of conversation and walks in cities but also reading a draft.

I grew up in a house filled with books and ideas; I live in that same house again with my own family. My parents, Anita and Alex Page, infused it with my first memories. Eve Weinbaum, who read and improved every paragraph in this book, created a new home in that place, with new layers of memory, for our children and for us.

why preservation matters

Old images die hard. When Americans think of Medellín, Colombia, they immediately picture street battles between drug lords and the police, war-torn neighborhoods, and rampant crime. That image is two decades out of date. Today, Medellín is well into a renaissance, anchored by visionary ideas about how to make a city safe and vibrant. Soon after I arrived with my family, the government and the Revolutionary Armed Forces of Colombia (FARC), the largest of the guerrilla forces that have been party to the longest civil war in South America, finally reached agreement in Havana, Cuba. After fifty years, after hundreds of thousands of people lost their lives and millions were displaced (only with Syria's mass refugee crisis of 2015 did Colombia lose its dubious place at the top of the list of countries with the most internally displaced people), after a drug war that added layers of terror and destruction to the guerrilla war, Colombia may finally experience peace and a chance for rebuilding and eventual reconciliation. Part of this rebuilding will be the work of preservationists. Now is the time when memory could play a crucial role in solidifying Colombia's new world, and contributing to reconciliation and social justice.

In fact, the process of reconciliation and rebuilding began in Medellín two decades ago, before the end of the war, with the death of the drug lord Pablo Escobar and the collapse of his cartel. This was Escobar's city; from my apartment in the El Poblado neighborhood I could almost see his home, where he held much of the city in his tight, sometimes generous, always violent, grip. In the hills of Medellín was La Catedral, his private prison, from where he could look over his beloved birthplace, which had become, thanks to him, a war zone.

There has been precious little preservation as we usually define it in Medellín. The city has few individual buildings of great beauty; neither is there a fabric of older buildings that invite care. But Medellín has for two decades pursued a new kind of preservation, a brand of "social urbanism" with the motto "Todos por la vida," "everything for life," aiming to reconstitute public life by restoring—I'd call it preserving—its public spaces as necessary components of healthy, peaceful civic life. Successive mayors, pressed by citizens, have built a modern public transportation system—the country's only rail metro system is here, not in the capital of Bogotá—and a network of "metro cables," gondolas that reach up into the steep, deeply poor and formerly violent neighborhoods. In one neighborhood, Comuna 13, elegant and safe outdoor escalators erase the isolation of thousands of residents in an area previously oppressed by drug trafficking. Across the city are two dozen new public libraries, sited at revived neigh-

Outdoor escalators in Comuna 13, Medellín, Colombia, 2015
In one of the poorest neighborhoods of Medellín, outdoor escalators, which
have linked residents to the metro system and jobs and thus helped stabilize
and rejuvenate a community victimized by violent battles between drug gangs
and the national army, symbolize the city's effort to make public life vital again.

borhood hubs, accompanied by new parks, walkways, and bridges designed to knit together previously divided neighborhoods.

And the citizens of Medellín have insisted that memory be a central project of the new city. Groups of survivors and mothers of victims have organized themselves over the past decades and are demanding information about their loved ones, genuine reparations, and the memorialization of sites associated with atrocity. At the Casa de la Memoria in downtown Medellín, which opened just a few years ago, the images of the victims and the voices of their family members are central. It is not a memorial and it is not a museum—it is a "house," where people gather to talk, to record, to learn, to engage. It was opened long before a peace treaty seemed likely. Its work has just begun.

In November 2015, the images of the carnage in Paris competed for space with discussions of the latest investigations into crimes by right-wing paramilitary groups in Colombia and anniversary memories of the 1985 attack on the Supreme Court building in the heart of Bogotá. But there were hopeful images as well: pictures from the turn of the twentieth century of the rue Bichat in the 10th arrondissement, site of one of the Paris massacres, that showed people walking along the streets, sitting in cafés, having dinner. The terrorists had interrupted, but could not destroy, what has been preserved through law and custom: cities of life and light.

Memory in the city, memory located in spaces and buildings, memory for building a better, more just city—all of this is in the air in Medellín, and lies in the spaces between the lines of this book.

I

not your grandmother's preservation movement

I was born in 1966, the year the modern historic preservation movement entered a new chapter with the passage of the National Historic Preservation Act. But I did not think much about preservation until college, when I took a course called "Modern Architecture," and watched Yale's great architectural historian Vincent Scully wield a ten-foot bamboo pole and pound a screen filled with images of New York's Pennsylvania Station in its heyday and today, after the original building was demolished and replaced by Madison Square Garden, with the station underneath it. He growled in anger, "We once entered the cities like gods, and now we scurry in like rats." Here was an open-and-shut case of architectural murder

Pennsylvania Station, New York City, 2007
Photographs from the 1930s by Berenice Abbott of McKim, Mead, and
White's glorious train station, which was torn down in the 1960s, adorn the
walls of the new, decidedly uninspiring underground station.

and its response: a movement of preservationists who declared,
"Never again," and who would stand in the way of the next
threatened landmark, and the next.[1]

That was yesterday's preservation movement. What is the
preservation movement becoming today?

In Amherst, Massachusetts, where I live, Emily Dickinson's
grave site shares attention with newly restored headstones of veterans of the Massachusetts 54th, the all–African American reg-
iment in the Civil War, who had long lain forgotten in a segre-
gated corner of the cemetery. Some of those men now take pride

Emily Dickinson Homestead, Amherst, Massachusetts, 2009
A National Historic Landmark, the Dickinson Homestead museum has
labored to balance a focus on innovative programs about the poet's writing
and the physical restoration of the building, including recent projects to
repaint the house in an approximation of its nineteenth-century color, and
remove a hundred century-old trees in order to re-create the lower hedge
Dickinson wrote about.

of place alongside the poet at the center of a hundred-foot-long mural of Amherst history overlooking the cemetery. Meanwhile, Dickinson's home, now a museum, is struggling successfully to move beyond the traditional focus on restoring the buildings and grounds, and instead welcoming innovative programs by artists and writers, to use the site as a springboard to new creativity.

In Holyoke, the preservation of the city's industrial heritage is couched not so much in aesthetic terms as in terms of climate change: by saving its sturdy nineteenth-century paper-industry buildings and taking advantage of the cheap clean energy produced by the 150-year-old canal system, the city is making preservation the means to a more economically vibrant and environmentally sustainable future.

In Boston, a community land trust created by the Dudley Street Neighborhood Initiative anchors affordable housing in the neighborhood. New transportation is bringing increased investment opportunities and easier access to downtown, but without the social upheaval caused by displacement and gentrification. Because the land trust holds the rights to the 225 homes it administers in perpetuity, it can keep them affordable and blunt the impact of gentrification. Few of these homes are architecturally distinguished, but as symbols of a different kind of preservation effort, they are extraordinary.

This is not your grandmother's preservation movement. In the fifty years since the passage of the preservation act, a lot has changed. But as in families, where children cannot escape their parents' and grandparents' DNA, the influence of those earlier

Dudley Square, Boston, 2013
The neighborhood is being stabilized to resist gentrification by Dudley
Neighbors, a community land trust that saves historic buildings but
maintains them as affordable housing in perpetuity.

preservationists continues to affect today's movement. The preservation world built by their ancestors is deeply rooted in Americans' cultural life, not to mention their laws and regulations. In some ways the sources of the early successes have become obstacles that will hold the movement back. The next generation must continue the work already begun of moving preservation in new directions.

The 1966 act established the National Register of Historic Places and the process by which individuals, cities, and states could add important places to it. Although a listing on the National Register does not guarantee preservation—and most towns can usually do little more than delay demolition of historic properties—the act represented an important step in the movement. It required that every state have a preservation officer; it spurred the creation of local historic commissions; and it established guidelines for standards of preservation and rehabilitation. Later legislation added tax incentives to encourage professional rehabilitation. The power to compel preservation is weak: only legally constituted historic districts, which are rare, have the power to restrict changes to buildings. But fifty years on, preservation is seen as an integral function of local government and a legitimate factor in community debates about land use.

The evidence of success is everywhere. There are now over a hundred thousand properties on the National Register. On Boston's Beacon Hill but also in the city's "Southie" neighborhood and the popular Quincy Market, in the industrial city of Lowell, and in small towns across the Commonwealth, houses and factories, public and private buildings have been saved and rehabilitated, and are now bringing in new investment. In Atlanta, not only has the capitol building been renovated; the defunct Fulton Bag and Cotton Mill has been refurbished into lofts and the nearby home of Dr. Martin Luther King, Jr., is a national historic site. Pike Place Market in Seattle, the Manzanar Japanese internment camp in California, worker housing in North Carolina, slave quarters in Mississippi, the Presidio in San Francisco, Latino homesteads in Colorado—all testify to a wider appreciation of the past nationwide, and the preservation movement deserves its share of credit for encouraging this broader view of what should be saved. The movement has also spurred a return to the city, and an appreciation of all its everyday glories: walkable neighborhoods, corner stores and row houses, the high density that is the foundation of a vibrant community. It is an impressive legacy.

And yet, filial piety should not prevent Americans from seeing that there are also some troubling issues with the U.S. preservation movement and the world it has created. Americans need to look honestly at their relationship to their physical past, and take note of what good has been achieved and what needs fixing.

Notwithstanding the examples of Amherst, Holyoke, and Dudley Street, the mainstream American preservation movement still remains focused on architecture—on saving what advocates consider beautiful and preventing the construction of what they consider ugly. The renewed preservation movement of the 1960s came in reaction to decades of massive urban renewal and a wholesale dismissal of the past. Its ideology arose, as the *New Yorker* architecture critic Paul Goldberger has written, "as much out of fear of what would be built as out of love for what people were trying to preserve."[2] In communities across the United States, preservationists' lofty ideals have too often degenerated into squabbles about the appearance of new windows and the color of shingles. Preservationists have too readily worked to protect the homes of wealthy people while allowing homes and neighborhoods of the working classes to be demolished, wiping away the layers of history that make places meaningful.

For much of the past fifty years, the U.S. preservation movement has been concerned primarily with places of celebratory history. Only recently has there been a push to preserve "difficult places," the sites where slavery or segregation, racial or other violence, even genocide, have taken place. An entire ecosystem has been built around the "curatorial management of the built environment," in the words of James Marston Fitch, one of the fathers of modern preservation, in which preservationists have emulated the museum approach to the conservation of precious objects. But what does that focus do to the history that is not about architectural gems? Is the site of the Shockoe Bottom slave market in downtown Richmond, Virginia, largely paved over by Interstate 95 and parking lots, to be ignored because it lacks the "integrity" that the secretary of the interior's standards for preservation identify as a requirement for listing on the National Register?

Scarred by the demolition of Pennsylvania Station (and versions of that debacle across the country), the U.S. preservation movement has done a lot to save old buildings and other monuments but surprisingly little to tell their stories. Few curators have engaged writers and artists to communicate the meanings of the places of architectural and historical significance they seek to preserve. They are more likely to invest in matching the original paint color than in creatively telling the history of the site and why it should matter to visitors today.

Not least, particularly in the United States, the preservation movement has too often become a handmaiden to real estate development that gives lip-service to the ideals of preservation in order to restore buildings that can be sold at huge cost to the wealthy. Preservation organizations celebrate the restoration of old homes, even when the entire community that once lived in the neighborhood has had to leave it to seek lower rents. The facades look spectacular, but the community is missing. Far too often preservation has been used as a tool for enshrining the inequality between rich and poor that is the stamp of our global age.

The good news is that although few people in the United States understand how preservation works, or could name a single law that governs preservation, most recognize that historic places matter, now more than ever. More people visit historic sites than read books of history. Historic buildings and landscapes are the open doors Americans walk through to enter the world of the past: to learn from it, to burnish old myths, to find a way to save their own towns and histories. As human beings, we are drawn to historic places. We believe in them. We crave them. They appeal to some of our deepest desires.

In this book I tell the story of why historic preservation has mattered in the past and why it should matter in new ways in the future. I focus on the United States but draw on past and present models from around the world to explore the variety of reasons individuals and communities have given for saving historic places, the difficult dilemmas that have plagued the U.S. preservation movement in particular—dilemmas that have sometimes led advocates to be party to inequities and repressive politics—and how the movement might become a force for social reform worldwide in the future. Preservation is not simply about the past; it can be the foundation for building more just communities for the future.

The story of the meaning of historic places cannot be told

in a tone of detachment. In this book I tell the stories of historic places that have meaning for individuals, as well as sites of national importance to which each individual brings his or her own meanings. The fate of my mother's dilapidated house in Camden, New Jersey, is a story from my personal history, but it is also a story at the heart of preservation—what does it mean to go home again? The $20 billion World Trade Center site project may be the focus of national mourning and mythmaking, but it is also where individuals come to experience a private emotional connection to an individual past. Preservation is impossible to understand without the stories of meaningful places—the celebratory, the uplifting, the beautiful, but also the painful, the shameful, and the divisive.

In Tony Kushner's play *Slavs!* the oldest living Bolshevik, Prelapsarianov, asks, "How are we to proceed without theory? Is it enough to reject the past, is it wise to move forward in this blind fashion, without the cold brilliant light of theory to guide the way? . . . You who live in this sour little age cannot imagine the sheer grandeur of the prospect we gazed upon."[3] Americans are in need of a compelling vision for the future of preservation, to return the "movement" part of their preservation movement. What might that vision be?

They might start by acknowledging the remarkable changes in the country over the past fifty years. The exciting, if uneven, developments we are seeing in preservation are products of a new world, unimaginable by the drafters of the 1966 law. The greatest wave of immigration to the United States—exceeding even the epic migrations of the late nineteenth century from China and southern and eastern Europe—was only just beginning. Millions of Asian and Latin American migrants have since joined the American polity, and they are now coalescing into major political and cultural forces, demanding their place at the table—and in the national story.

Economic inequality in 1966 was in decline, the product of postwar economic growth, strong unions, and President Lyndon Johnson's War on Poverty policies. No one would have predicted that fifty years later inequality would be as great as during the rapacious Gilded Age of the late nineteenth century, and that neoliberal economic policies would be enthroned, despite all evidence of their destructive effects. When Jane Jacobs advocated preserving the small blocks and tenement buildings of her Greenwich Village neighborhood in *The Death and Life of Great American Cities,* she assumed the continuance of a broad middle class as well as public investments that could maintain a mixed-income neighborhood far into the future. She could not have predicted that her neighborhood would become home to a new elite, with her own modest home from the 1950s lovingly preserved by law—but selling for millions.

The early environmental movements were focused on the destruction of the natural environment—the emission of pollution by smokestacks, the dumping of toxic garbage. But big cars and thirty-cents-a-gallon gas were the norm, and virtually no one was thinking about what we might be doing to the earth's atmosphere, or recognizing that the effects of policies, both in the United States and abroad, would be felt within a few short decades. Preservation was concerned with beauty and buildings, not an unknown problem that would come to be called climate change.

A progressive preservation movement must address the problems of this new world.

For preservation to flourish it cannot be solely about architecture. The early nineteenth-century preservationists cared primarily about saving their own history, even if the history they celebrated was narrowly focused and served clear political purposes. Only when we place a comprehensive understanding of history and communal meaning at the center of preservation work will the movement tell the full story of a diverse world. Rather than ask, "What style is this house?" we should ask, as Tom Mayes of the National Trust has done, "Why do old places matter?"[4] Within the preservation movement, reams have been written about the practice of repairing and rehabilitating historic structures—technologies, techniques, materials—but little of those discussions will show up in these pages. As important as those issues may be, they already have the lion's share of attention in the world of preservation. In this book I look beyond the practices of conservation work to the role of preservation as a force in public life.

In addition, saving historic places and reusing them must be a cornerstone of environmental sustainability. Nearly half of all greenhouse gases are produced in the construction, demolition, and operation of commercial and residential buildings. We need to find ways that the preservation movement can join the conservation movement to achieve more sustainable communities. For the preservation movement to fully embrace its role in the fight against global warming, we must jettison some of our concern with aesthetics. We must change what we mean by "value" in old places. We need to save and reuse even "ugly" old buildings because demolishing and replacing them contributes to the problem of climate change.

A sustainability ethos ask us to abandon the conservator's approach to architectural "integrity" and widen our focus to a far greater range of old buildings with their layers of old and new, interwoven in a single building or landscape. Paradoxically, progress requires that we re-adopt older ideas: that we look at sites in terms of layers of time, that we are more flexible about what constitutes "authenticity" or "integrity," and that we value the architecture of adaptive reuse, just as our forebears did. Preservationists around the world are looking back to go forward, adapting ideas from other cultures to enrich their own.

At the same time, we will have to broaden what we mean by preserving history. One of the most exciting developments in historic preservation in the past quarter century has been the growing interest in understanding the pain that inheres in difficult places, places of suffering and national disgrace, and what have been called "sites of conscience." From Richmond to Berlin, Mountain Meadows, Utah, to Buenos Aires, preservationists are restoring and reinterpreting difficult places of the past for future generations. To help create greater unity in a stunningly diverse nation of immigrants, the U.S. preservation movement must bring Americans face to face with the legacies of their controversial pasts. This courageous approach has already begun, infusing new life into the preservation movement by spurring dialogue at places like the Tenement Museum in New York City, the Manzanar Japanese-American internment camp, and newly interpreted slave plantations across the South.

Perhaps most thorny of all, the new movement cannot be a tool of gentrifiers but a means of achieving economically just communities. If we care about creating dense, and thus more sustainable, cities and towns, but reject the reorganization of cities by class, we will have to offer a new model for saving buildings and communities. This means embracing public housing as well as new forms of property ownership such as community land trusts and cooperative housing as a way to protect against the dislocations of market-based private investment. It means passing local ordinances such as the one in San Francisco that helps support long-standing community businesses, and restoring dilapidated structures as the basis for local economic development. And it means putting the "movement" back in the preservation movement by taking to the streets to protest the displacement of our neighbors. When the Boston grassroots organization City Life conducts acts of civil disobedience to prevent low-income residents from being evicted from their neighborhoods by multinational banks, they are acting as preservationists. Traditional preservation organizations should stand with them.

This is preservation's moment. The movement can finally free itself from the stigma of being aesthetically elitist, of being the domain of the rich, of standing in the way of progress, of being obsessed with architecture. And it can find itself offering solutions to some of the most pressing problems of our world—crafting a sustainable approach to climate change, honestly confronting our difficult pasts, and reclaiming a more equitable society.

2 why we preserve

On your way to see the Emily Dickinson Homestead (a major reason visitors come to Amherst, Massachusetts), a National Historic Landmark and the place where the poet used to draw inspiration on her own "old Grounds of memory," you would be forgiven for walking right by the dusty northwest corner of the Town Common. At one end of an ill-conceived parking lot bitten out of the grassy heart of the town, otherwise nobly framed by the buildings of Amherst College and the Richardsonian Town Hall, this corner hardly seems like a place worth remembering.[1]

For me, gazing at this ragged edge of the Amherst Town Common is like peering into a Technicolor well, rippling with my own past. In 1966 the Amherst Com-

Town Common, Amherst, Massachusetts,
Eyes Wide Open Iraq War Exhibition, 2004
The Amherst Common has been used as a gathering place for political action
for generations. This antiwar traveling exhibition featured the boots of
U.S. soldiers who died in Iraq.

mon Peace Vigil began, held on Sundays from noon to one o'clock without fail into the early 1970s; it was one of the longest-running protests against the Vietnam War in the country. The tradition of protest in Amherst has waxed and waned, but to this day our own version of London's Hyde Park Speakers' Corner draws protestors of all types to make their assorted pleas to passing motorists and pedestrians at the town's main intersection. I can see myself there, on my father's shoulders, as he strolled back and forth, smiling, with a pipe in his mouth. The image I have may be a memory constructed from family stories or the black-and-white photographs stuck into the fat albums that lined my childhood home. Memory is no "sacred Closet," as Emily called it (townspeople are on a first-name basis with the poet), no solid object leaning on the wall unchanging, gathering dust. Memory is more like the "reverential Broom" she mused about, whisking words and images, sounds and smells together to construct an emotion-filled scene.

My memory of sitting atop my father's shoulders—the shoulders that are now visibly shrunken in his ninety-third year—has not resonated throughout my life with a consistent glow. No, this memory has grown stronger as my father has declined and as my own activism has increased. Recalling that day as I stand at this piece of ground both gives me back my father at the height of his full, ebullient life and serves as a foundation for my own political efforts today.

I learned a few years ago that the town had placed a memorial plaque in the ground. For a long time I could not find it, for it was covered with dirt, as though no one cared enough to keep the plaque clean or the memory alive. But now it strikes me that the dirt-covered plaque is as innovative a memorial as any I could imagine. It becomes visible again only when people are marching and protesting on the Common, kicking away the dirt while awakening outrage. When that happens it reminds us of why we are there, at this very spot, still working to heal a broken world.

Most of us understand why the Emily Dickinson Homestead matters; Dickinson was one of America's greatest poets, and she was inspired by the house she lived in, the gardens that surrounded it, and the people who visited. Few writers are as connected to a place as Emily Dickinson was to the town of Amherst; preserving the home where the poet lived, which has now become a museum, so that future generations might gain new insight to and connection with her poetry, is a crucial reason preservation matters today.

But that scrappy corner of the Amherst Town Common also matters, not just to me, as part of my own personal identity, but to the town, as part of its identity, and to those who visit it because of Amherst's reputation as a home of liberal politics. The sight of people making a stand together on that Common against the ongoing destruction of Syria, the various wars in Iraq, or gun violence, or in favor of progressive income taxes or single-payer health care, sustains activists today, for in them we can see the continuity of history.

"A society, first of all, needs landmarks," wrote the sociologist Maurice Halbwachs in the 1930s.[2] Memory is impossible without society—families, communities, nations—but it is also impossible without physical places on which to ground it, for they bear witness to past events. The creation of landmarks does not require an architect. The most powerful sites of personal memory are often the anonymous places that are given their meaning by individuals.

Why do we preserve old places? The reasons are many, and have evolved in recent decades. We preserve for personal and collective memory, to anchor individual identity and national

Chatham Square Cemetery, Lower East Side, New York, 2002
Behind the tenements of Chinatown stands a powerful visual reminder of the
layers of history in New York: one of the oldest extant human-made places
on Manhattan Island, the 1682 cemetery of Shearith Israel, the first Jewish
congregation in New Amsterdam.

truths and myths, to secure a place in the river of time, to spur our imaginations. Such preservation serves a true and meaningful function for individuals and communities. But we have become increasingly invested in preservation, which suggests that we preserve in pursuit of even deeper needs that we think can be secured by a physical connection to the past. If we wish to shape a vision for the future of preservation we need to understand the many notes of its call.

The context for the 1966 National Historic Preservation Act was the rapid expansion of America's cities and suburbs and the unrelenting demolition of centuries-old buildings and landscapes in favor of towers and suburban homes, highways and malls. The works of Rachel Carson, Jane Jacobs, and J. B. Jackson bore powerful witness to the desecration of the American landscape. These writers belonged to and built on a tradition that had solidified in early-twentieth-century discussions of the rapid growth of American cities. Private and public elites in New York City, for example, became consumed with the problem of destruction and preservation. For many, the destruction of the old and its replacement by the new was visible proof of the greatness of the city. And because New York was often treated as the stand-in for the United States more generally, the city of "creative destruction," in the words of the midcentury economist Joseph Schumpeter, symbolized America's unstoppable rise.[3] Only by destroying the old, the outdated, and the passé, and replacing it with the new, the modern, and the cutting edge would America keep the capitalist engine revving. "Why should we preserve anything?" seemed a reasonable question. But others, while thrilling in (and profiting from) the relentless tearing down and rebuilding, sensed that something profound was being lost with the fall of each building that had hosted an important event, represented a certain style, or could teach lessons about America to the thousands of new immigrants coming through Ellis Island every day.

The National Historic Preservation Act was an attempt to provide a clear set of answers to the question Why preserve? The "spirit and direction of the Nation," in the opening words of the act, "are founded upon and reflected in its historic heritage" and thus must be saved for future generations of Americans, so that they might have a "sense of orientation" and gain "cultural, aesthetic, inspirational, economic, and energy benefits" from the "preservation of this irreplaceable heritage." Section 1 is clear that the act is necessary because of the "ever-increasing extensions of urban centers, highways, and residential, commercial, and industrial developments," and that current programs and powers are "inadequate" to protect "the rich heritage of the Nation" for future generations.[4]

The register of motives codified by the National Historic Preservation Act remains the foundation for the arguments made by individuals and communities in favor of preservation. But preservationists have also steadily modified and added to the justifications.

We all can instinctively name a number of reasons for preserving historic places. In a series of blog posts created during a fellowship at the American Academy in Rome, Tom Mayes of the National Trust for Historic Preservation produced a thorough and eloquent list of fourteen that encompasses some that have only recently been promoted.[5] He includes on his list values we might readily acknowledge—the preservation of beauty, architecture, history. Just as we seek the beautiful in art of all ages, so too we look to—and hope to be able to return to—the most aesthetically pleasing and important places from the past. But we "revere old buildings," Mayes argues, just as much for their "art and craftsmanship," their ability to reveal the skills and commitment of past times.[6] Old places help us, as well, Mayes argues, connect to historical events in visceral ways that books, images, or documents typically do not (although we might all imagine a particular image or historic document that evokes a powerful connection or insight). Preservation can reveal the physical manifestations of our history, including events and episodes and structures that go against contemporary values. Through historic preservation, we can see the world we have created. Although we must beware of a facile belief in "time-machine" thinking—that we can imagine ourselves transported back in time when we encounter an old place—there is an undeniable power attached to the sites of past events.

But Mayes touches on these most readily acknowledged reasons for preservation only later in his series. He begins with what he sees as the core purposes of preservation: continuity, memory and identity. We gravitate to "old places" (he rightly shies away from insider terms like "historic resource" and is eager to move beyond talking only about buildings) in large measure because we seek a link, even a distant connection, between the past and present. To stand in the Roman Forum, or before the cliff houses in Canyon de Chelly in Arizona, is to find yourself, even without specific knowledge of the place, confronting the idea of the long sweep of time, grasping the most profound of historical lessons: people have lived, loved, fought, and raised families on this very spot. In cities that have endured through history, the historian and critic Lewis Mumford wrote, "time becomes visible."[7] Or as the filmmaker and photographer Wim Wenders said fifty years later, "A city does not tell you a story, but it reveals history. Cities do that in different ways: some make their history visible, others rather hide it. They can open your eyes, like movies, or they can close them. They can leave you abused, or they can nourish your imagination."[8]

Continuity without connection to the meanings embodied in old places is not sufficient. Mayes rightly argues that we live within identities formed at the individual, group, and (especially in the past several centuries) national levels, and thus often through interaction with old places. Preservation touches on our personal memories, linking us to our own past, and taps into our desire to connect with people of different places and times.

The Lincoln Memorial provides a good example of how personal and collective identities are tied to historic sites. The memorial was designed to make visitors think of Lincoln and his ideals, the Civil War, the lives lost, the union preserved. But it was built in 1922 as part of the continuing effort to reunite white southerners with white northerners; in the memorial the union is the message, not the end of slavery. The Lincoln Memorial became a landmark in the struggle for racial equality only after it was used as one. In 1939 the singer Marian Anderson sang on

Lincoln Memorial, Washington, D.C., 2016
A monument designed to build unity between white leaders from the North
and South, with little reference to slavery, the Lincoln Memorial became a
symbol of the struggle for civil rights owing to its deliberate appropriation by
black activists such as Marian Anderson and Martin Luther King, Jr.

its steps after she was denied a booking at Constitution Hall,
owned by the Daughters of the American Revolution, and on
August 28, 1963, Martin Luther King, Jr., delivered his "I Have
a Dream" speech on the monument's steps. In addition, many
Americans also have a personal connection to the monument as
a point of reference for other political marches. Americans need
the Lincoln Memorial, not only as a reminder of past events
shaping their national identity, but as a gathering place for debate about the future of that identity.[9]

Mayes also discusses reasons for preservation that have assumed greater importance in recent years. He points to the growing belief (which I'll discuss in Chapter 4) that we must save old places because it makes good economic sense. Similarly, the creative economy—artists, writers, theater groups—and even creative inspiration itself, he argues, are nourished by old places. Places where great musicians have recorded their music, sites where artists worked, can inspire new generations of artists. Old places have a special capacity to inspire creative thinking, in part because of the combination of artistic aspiration embodied in buildings and landscapes and in part because of the layers of life that have taken place within their walls, or on their streets, or across their fields. An old home, the philosopher Gaston Bachelard reminded us, "shelters daydreaming, the house protects the dreamer, the house allows one to dream in peace."[10]

Each of these arguments captures one of the varied reasons people today seek to preserve old places. But a few questions lurk beneath the surface: Why do we adopt this particular set of justifications for historic preservation now, in the early twenty-first century? Why are we preserving more places, and immersing ourselves in the past in new ways—memorializing more events, building more museums, delving deeper and more widely into genealogy, creating bigger archives? Our time is defined by an "abundance of heritage," writes the archaeologist and heritage theorist Rodney Harrison. "Heritage is ubiquitous."[11]

Why has there been an explosion of interest in memory making in its many forms, and historic preservation in particular, since the last decades of the twentieth century? The frenetic intensity to immerse ourselves in emblems of the past has to make us ask, What is driving us? What is the urge that lies beneath our undertaking?

This conundrum defines our memory crisis: the sense that, in Marx's words, "all that is solid melts into air," that we inhabit lives without clear foundations in spirit, in time, in values, or in a meaningful past, and consequently, we seek to ground ourselves by creating "sites of memory," in the words of the historian Pierre Nora, or what the historian Yosef Hayim Yerushalmi calls "vessels and vehicles of memory"—in memorials and photograph archives, in oral histories and scholarly monographs, in museums and historic buildings, in landscapes.[12] Although people describe the United States as a forgetful nation, young and uninterested in the past, the explosion of museums, memorials, and historic sites, and the emphasis on historic preservation, suggests otherwise.

We live in a world filled with sites of memory, but we no longer inhabit *milieux de mémoire,* "environments of memory," as Nora calls them with more than a hint of nostalgia, that provided meaning for people in the past. We cannot. Even for those with strong religious beliefs, modern sensibilities militate against a complete immersion in sacred beliefs. We cannot escape the world we have created, which includes beliefs in liberty and democracy, scientific rationalism and religious skepticism, a world which has released people from the bonds of tradition and community, but left us without moorings. Here is the fundamental dilemma: We are modern people; we cannot return to the past. And yet, we still crave the security we associate with the past. As the philosopher Franz Rosenzweig said nearly a century ago: "There is no one today who is not alienated."[13] The philosopher Karsten Harries, a half century later, wrote similarly: "The reward of this displacement is a new freedom, its price a new homelessness."[14]

Our contemporary debates about the value of history versus the importance of memory, the prestige of myth and personal recollection versus the alleged science of professional history, go to the heart of this dilemma. History, David Lowenthal, a pioneer in the field of heritage studies, has written, is at war with "heritage," because they both seek rights over the past, but the two have different missions. History seeks to explain, heritage to make meaning. Pierre Nora puts it even more bluntly: "History is perpetually suspicious of memory, and its true mission is to suppress and destroy it."[15]

The traffic jam of the many "vehicles of memory," in Yerushalmi's words, reflects our effort to find a way between history and heritage. The architect Rem Koolhaas in a provocative essay complains that "preservation is overtaking us" and imagines a time when we will landmark a building before it is even completed. Koolhaas astutely recognizes that preservation is not a foreign invader seeking to undermine modernity. Rather, as he writes, "preservation is not the enemy of modernity but actually one of its inventions."[16] Preservation—and the other memory projects we are busy creating—is not an undertaking left over from a premodern time. Preservation as a project involving scientific analysis, rational justifications for value, organizations and commissions, is something that could only be born of the modern world.

The proliferation of national and state historic preservation registers reflects the work of many forces, including the growing diversity of the United States and the insistence that the stories of all its immigrants and ethnic and racial minorities must be told in public. It reflects a concern for economic development in a neoliberal economy. It reflects anxiety over climate change. It reflects the fear that as increasing numbers have returned to cities over the past thirty years, the country is losing its distant and more recent physical heritage, just as city dwellers worried about how the rise of the great metropolises of the nineteenth and twentieth centuries would affect their culture.

But such concerns only touch the surface. Martin Heidegger, in one of his first postwar writings (having been effectively silenced for his support for the Nazi regime), a lecture in 1951 at a Darmstadt housing convention, pushed his audience to consider whether the need for roofs over peoples' heads was not the most pressing question facing war-torn Germany. Rather, what haunted him was the sense that we had lost the sense of what it meant to *dwell*. "However hard and bitter, however hampering and threatening the lack of houses remains," Heidegger claimed, "the *real plight of dwelling* does not lie merely in a lack of houses. The real plight of dwelling is indeed older than the world wars with their destruction, older also than the increase of the earth's population and the condition of the industrial workers. The real dwelling plight lies in this, that mortals ever search anew for the nature of dwelling, that they *must ever learn to dwell*."[17] If we build only roofs and bedrooms, we have not responded to our deeper need, a need as essential as shelter from the elements. At the deepest level, we are trying to recover connections that we or our parents or our grandparents lost. We have an "aching nostalgia," says Yerushalmi, for a vanished past. And while we may trust historians and be committed to living much of our lives according to historical fact and evidence, we "patently do not want the past that is offered by the historian."[18]

What we are looking for is a soul-deep connection to our world, and preservation has offered a means by which we hope to find it: through the allegedly pure encounter with the physical past. Part of my frustration with architectural preservation is precisely that I believe that one of the central concepts underpinning contemporary historic preservation is deeply suspect: the concept of authenticity.

If there is anything a city such as Rome teaches clearly and convincingly, day after day, it is that architectural "authenticity" is a mirage and a chimera, unrealistic and a delusion, something we only imagine exists. Every building we deem to be "in its original state" or "perfectly preserved" is simply not. In Rome, buildings are created from pieces of previous buildings—a church is built upon an earlier church, which was erected upon a villa or temple. The Acqua Paola, the glorious baroque fountain a hundred yards from the American Academy, where I lived for six months, is, like many other Renaissance buildings, largely made of spolia (repurposed building material) from classical Roman buildings. Rome is about recycling. Ruins have been covered and uncovered, they have been rearranged, their contexts have been altered by new buildings, new roads, dirt and garbage, pollution and graffiti. To insist on the pursuit of the "authentic," which is often

Fontana dell'Acqua Paola, Janiculum Hill, Rome, 2014
The glorious Acqua Paola was built in 1612, largely of marble taken from nearby Roman temples.

presented as the "original," and to demand "integrity" of our historic buildings is a fools' errand, a fetishizing of the past that does violence to the past itself as well as to the present.

These long-standing concerns about this central term in preservation theory and practice are beautifully discussed in Richard Todd's *The Thing Itself,* which is centered around our common quest for authentic objects, places, experiences, and relationships.[19] At the beginning of his book Todd describes buying a small wooden box at one of the largest antique markets in the United States, in Brimfield, Massachusetts. He was drawn to a small box that the dealer claimed was almost two hundred years old, and paid a good chunk of change for it. Setting it on the front passenger seat as he drove to visit a friend, he continued to glance at his cherished new purchase, but gradually he began to feel a sense of discomfort about it. When he arrived at the home of his friend, an expert in material culture, his suspicions were confirmed: the box was a fake.

Todd tells another story about his house, which, the records prove, dates to the eighteenth century. After he decided to replace its modern windows, he was thrilled to find someone in his area who was getting rid of his own eighteenth-century windows. Todd eagerly bought them and installed them in his house, pleased that he had "authentically" rehabilitated his home. He had been a good steward to the past. But there remained a nagging doubt. He had taken windows from another building and inserted them, like a surgeon, into his own. His house was not "original" anymore; it had become an artifice of sorts. The windows were "authentic" but not authentic to his particular house. Passersby might marvel at the completeness of the mid-1700s house, but what they were looking at was a composite, something rigged to look complete.

In both episodes, Todd was searching for something "real" in a world that he saw as unmoored from reality, dedicated to fabrication. His book uncovers his dawning awareness that the search might always be elusive. It also hearkens back to a study by the literary critic Lionel Trilling, *Sincerity and Authenticity,* which arose from a series of lectures in 1970. Trilling trawls through much of Western history and literature to ask why "at a certain point in history certain men and classes of men conceived that the making of this effort [to be sincere] was of supreme importance in the moral life, and the value they attached to the enterprise of sincerity became a salient, perhaps a definitive, characteristic of Western culture for some four hundred years." He notes that "there have been cultural epochs in which men did not think of themselves as having a variety of selves or roles." There was a powerful backlash against the very idea of sincerity in the nineteenth century. Indeed, the quest for sincerity was seen by many on both sides of the Atlantic as the height of arrogance and the clearest sign of, ironically, insincerity. As diverse thinkers as Emerson and Nietzsche had a "principled antagonism to sincerity," and "both spoke in praise of what they call the mask." Emerson put it bluntly in 1840: "There is no deeper dissembler than the sincerest man." Oscar Wilde not only condemned the quest for sincerity but embraced the falseness of public presentation, claiming that "the first duty in life is to be as artificial as possible . . . what the second duty is no one has yet discovered."[20]

Trilling was writing from the vantage point of the early 1970s, when artifice and insincerity were not valued, but condemned, and his purpose was to shine a historical light on the terms bandied about at the time, to suggest the dark underside to glorifying the slippery ideas of sincerity and authenticity. He linked the idea of sincerity to the British polymath John Ruskin, who, among many other projects, laid out the foundational principles of the modern preservation movement in Great Britain and was an inspiration to William Morris and the arts and crafts movement at the end of the nineteenth century. Ruskin's views were the intellectual source of what Morris would call the "anti-scrape" philosophy of architectural preservation. To Ruskin, the greatest buildings were those, like cathedrals, that were built over time, and emerged "organically" from their civilizations. They were to be cherished as a vital link to a past. They should not be added to, or restored, because we in the modern world could not reproduce the culture and craftsmanship that had produced them. Better to leave the buildings to slowly decline than taint them with corrupted modern hands.[21]

For some modernists, Ruskin, with his emphasis on restoring dignity to the lives of working people and wiping away the artifice of nineteenth-century manners and tastes, was an inspiration. But for others, especially the Italian futurists—the most eloquent, aggressive, and ultimately violent of the early-twentieth-century modernists—he was hopelessly and dangerously backward. For Filippo Marinetti, father of the futurist movement, Ruskin was the enemy, the symbol of all that was weak, "lympathic" about England and more broadly European culture: "With his sick dream of a primitive pastoral life: with his nostalgia for Homeric cheese and legendary spinning-wheels; with his hatred of the machine, of steam and electricity, this maniac for antique simplicity resembles a man who in full maturity wants to sleep in his cot again and drink at the breasts of a nurse who has now grown old."[22]

What Ruskin lacked, critics like Marinetti argued, was not sincerity but rather a quality with a far greater "moral intensity," characterized by a "censorious tone" and animated by a call to "rigor." For Marinetti, what the world needed was muscular authenticity. And *authenticity,* a word that gained potency as the

twentieth century wore on, was, to Trilling's mind, a dangerous goal. *Authenticity* is derived from the Greek word *authenteo,*
which means both "to have full power over" and "to commit a
murder." The *authentes* is "not only a master, a doer, but also a
perpetrator, a murderer, even a self-murderer, a suicide." Martin
Heidegger argued in his essay "Building, Dwelling, Thinking"
that the echoes of original meanings of words live on and rumble
beneath the surface of our contemporary usage. The aggressive,
violent resonances of *authenticity* remain present on our tongues
and in our synapses. And that should give us pause. One dan-
ger in the ideal of authenticity is the certainty that lies within
the word and the concept as it is applied to preservation. There
is no "partial" authenticity. A place is either authentic or it is
not. *Authenticity* has been employed to make black-and-white
distinctions, and in historic preservation to mask the layers of
history that exist in almost all places.[23]

I cannot help in this context but think of Walter Benjamin's
influential, difficult essay "The Work of Art in the Age of Mechanical Reproduction." The epilogue to the piece, written in 1936,
focuses on fascism and its relationship to art. Benjamin, like
Trilling, quotes Marinetti on his embrace of war—"war is beautiful."[24] It is a puzzling ending. How has he moved from new
ways of printing photographs to fascism? The issue is not a sim-
plistic one. Benjamin was arguing far beyond the question of art
and the machines of reproduction. He was suggesting that our
technology had leapt far beyond our ability to comprehend it or
manage it. Our notions of aesthetics and so much else had been
upset by industrialization and proletarianization—by machinery

that we had turned to new avenues of aesthetic pleasure. Fascism and war were, in a disturbing way, endemic to our quest for a new, and, yes, authentic feeling.

To suggest that the quest for authenticity in preservation is fascist is, of course, ridiculous. But if we step back from that intellectual cliff we might suggest something less shocking but still disturbing in the relationship between notions of personal and societal authenticity and the authenticity of a historic building or site: we crave in a historic building an authenticity that we don't have elsewhere in our lives. This may explain why authenticity rises and falls as a value in preservation. When we seek in the external world—in people, in buildings, and in landscapes—that which we crave internally, there is bound to be a disjunction. The intensity of the quest for the authentic in historic places is born out of our own sense—perhaps fundamental, as Freud argued, and perhaps heightened in our own individual social settings—of our own lack of authenticity. And that is a dangerous mix.

Perhaps by battling against accepted notions of the "authentic" in preservation we might assist ourselves, as individuals and as a society, to abandon this unending, and always unsuccessful, quest.

David Cromer's production of Thornton Wilder's *Our Town* had a much-praised run at the Barrow Street Theater in Greenwich Village in 2009. As prescribed by Wilder there was "No curtain. No scenery." "The play is called 'Our Town,'" says the Stage Manager in the opening lines. "It was written by Thornton Wilder. . . . The name of the town is Grover's Corners, New Hampshire—just across the Massachusetts line: latitude 42 degrees 40 minutes; longitude 70 degrees 37 minutes."[25] The hint of an underlying theme related to architecture, community, and place is already present in the opening lines. Is this place, Grover's Corners, defined by its geographical location? Of course not. It will be defined by people, their loves and losses, their memories.

In Cromer's production, the audience (I was one) surrounded the stage, sitting just inches from the actors. It was stark in its sparseness: a stage occupied by a few tables and chairs, which were set up by the Stage Manager as the audience trickled in. As the evening wore on, the audience began to feel the emptiness of the town as a physical place. An hour into the drama we had been pulled into a world composed of words and relationships, and we had forgotten about physical place. In the third act, young Emily Webb, now dead, sits in a chair—a stand-in for a coffin—in the graveyard with her mother-in-law and other deceased townspeople. She prays for and is granted a chance to return to one day in her life. She chooses the morning of her twelfth birthday in her childhood home. Suddenly the black curtain at the back of the theater is pulled open to show, magically, a perfect re-creation of the family in their kitchen on that long-ago day, with period clothing, curtains, dishes, and furniture. Bacon is frying in the pan. The rich, colorful light and scenery, the sound of the meat sizzling, that deep, animal smell wafting into the theater—was overpowering. For the character Emily, it is as well. She is drawn in but then collapses in her newfound pain as she realizes that she cannot communicate with her family, and soon must return to her permanent home in the cemetery.

Only when Emily is offered the chance to go back—to remember, in the hope of returning or recovering—are we, the audience, brought into the physical world of textures and light and smell, and we are reminded that memory can be much more powerful and lifelike than material reality. If we are not careful, the present will come to us in black and white, and the past will be in full color. It is a strange fire, this power of old places. When preservationists save a place, they may be offering people a way to go back in time or to another way of seeing the world, to smell the bacon sizzling. But they might also be re-creating the dreams of the dead, confined to their cemeteries, anguishing over what they failed to appreciate while alive.

Confronting the deeper reasons of why we preserve is crucial to developing a preservation ethos for the future. For if the arguments we offer for preservation are only surface shouts of a deeper craving, and if those cravings cannot easily be met, if we seek a lost community of memory and can never secure it, what purpose does preservation serve?

Historic preservation is fundamentally about bringing old places and living people into contact and dialogue. Old places are powerful, and can spur our imagination, our emotions, our sense of connectedness in ways other connections to the past cannot. But this power can be dangerous, leading us to fetishistically focus on preserving the physical fabric of a place as if the past and its emotional and ethical lessons lay in the form. An emphasis on authenticity has led us to believe that we can time travel, that we can experience the lives of people in the past by standing before the places they built. It has at times led us to believe that if we honor the original we might recover a lost world and its values.

But what if we confront this fundamental dilemma of being modern people and embrace what preservation can really do? Perhaps we need to look elsewhere for the importance of preservation: its ability to help us confront a difficult past fully and honestly, to employ historic places in the service of economic justice, to secure a sustainable world, and to reaffirm beauty as a path to justice.

3

how americans preserve

How do Americans save old places from destruction?

Not easily. In defiance of a powerful commitment to private property. With little support from government or business. And mainly through individual advocacy and through a hodgepodge of local, state, and federal laws and agencies. And this is the situation *after* the National Historic Preservation Act of 1966 was passed, creating a more organized, government-led approach to preservation.

The simple premise of this chapter—how Americans preserve—belies the complicated laws and regulations that make the country's system of historic preservation one of remarkable achievements and confounding obstacles, dilemmas, and contradictions. While Ameri-

My childhood and current home in Amherst, Massachusetts, 2015
The house was built in 1916 with no known architect; it was probably
designed and constructed by a local builder.

cans might long for a system that has clarity and power, what has
been put in place is something of a Rube Goldberg contraption,
which, like those convoluted imaginary machines, has produced
some impressive final results but also led to other problems being
ignored while requiring a lot of grease and tinkering.

To help us understand this marvelous bureaucratic apparatus, let's start with an example of how someone might set about
preserving a building in the United States at the beginning of
the twenty-first century. How might I, for example, preserve my
own house?

Let's say that I one day decide that my house deserves to be
recognized and preserved for future generations. Or that a neighborhood group (like the one that formed in protest when a barn
allegedly used by the poet Robert Frost was torn down) decides
that my house and others like it need to be protected. The logical

thing would be to get the house, or perhaps the whole neighborhood, listed on the National Register of Historic Places. Why? Well, as a "national" list, it would, by including my house, suggest that it had national importance (even if it were approved as being of "local" significance). Second, almost every aspect of preservation—regulations, protective restrictions, funding—is based on a building, property, or site being on or at least eligible for listing on the National Register.

I would begin by filling out the appropriate nomination form for the National Register. This might require hiring a professional historic preservation consultant, as some of the questions require exact dimensions of the building and property and detailed location data (including a U.S. Geological Survey map), and others call for descriptions couched in architectural terminology. On these forms I will need to describe the property, using an architectural classification system and narrative description. For my house, I'd say that it was a typical four-square house, with Greek-inspired elements, such as Doric columns and entablature, as well as a front porch and back and side yards. I'd lay out all the dimensions of the house and property.

The nomination form also requires me to justify the significance of the place under one or more of four categories: significance to the town or nation's history; because of association with an important individual; as architecture; or for the possible archaeological information that could be revealed. In choosing my justifications I'd also need to explain the period of significance—during what part of its hundred-year history was the building "significant"? I'd have to say that I have no record of an architect working on my house and that it was probably constructed by a local builder; it is a typical solid early-twentieth-century New England home. I'd declare the "era of significance" as the year that it was built, 1916, since the history of my family living in it for more than fifty years does not qualify as having "association with the lives of persons significant in our past," no matter how much I might disagree. More likely, given the modest importance of my house, I might make my nomination part of a "multiple property" listing, and make the case for the whole neighborhood's significance, rather than resting my hopes on my one house. Of course, if I wanted to do that, I'd need the approval of a majority of my neighbors, and I'd have to fill out a different set of forms.

Once I complete the form (or forms), the standard practice is to submit it to the state historic preservation officer, whose office was mandated by the National Historic Preservation Act. To garner greater support, individuals or groups usually seek approval of a local historic commission, if their town has one. The state historic preservation officer will usually submit the nomination form to the state historic commission, which he or she leads. The commission's approval—or disapproval—will hold great weight with the Keeper of the National Register of Historic Places, who is the final arbiter of which historic places are given National Register status.

If approved by the Keeper, I will have the honor of placing a bronze plaque on my house that identifies it as being on the National Register. I will also retain the right to tear down my house the next day. Listing on the National Register in itself offers no protection to a building. Only in places where a city has created a designated "local historic district," with property-policing powers designated by the state, can restrictions be placed on changes made to the exterior. One of the few other powers, granted not by the federal government but states and localities, is to delay demolition of an important building for up to year, if the local ordinance allows. And if I want to keep my house, or even restore it to its original glory? There are precious few resources available. Some cities and towns have modest grants, or offer revolving loan funds. The one major source of funds is the federal tax credit, which is limited to income-producing properties, and thus essentially rules out owner-occupied homes.[1]

Of course, much historic preservation in the United States occurs without the National Register process. It is done by state and federal agencies that own thousands of historic structures. It is done by individual homeowners, out of necessity or pride, and without any support from the state or federal government. It is done by commercial property owners, who might decide that a historic building is ideal for a new restaurant, say, perhaps because its age and architectural details give it character. The majority of preservation happens beyond the scope of local historic districts, without involving the National Register, and without the use of public funds.

How well has this system served the country? A tragic loss in Chicago suggests some of its weaknesses.

The image is painful to look at: aging blues singer Jimmie Lee Robinson walking to the middle of Maxwell Street on Chicago's near east side in 2000 to sing "Maxwell Street Teardown Blues" as demolition crews tore down a block of buildings that framed what was once one of the most vibrant places of cultural creativity in America. In the 1940s and 1950s, Maxwell Street, with its many Jewish merchants and bustling market, became, with the arrival of waves of African American migrants from the South, the birthplace of the urban electric blues, a place where Muddy Waters, Robert Nighthawk, Little Walter, Hound Dog Taylor, and many other musicians had their start and where they turned an African American musical form into the foundation of a national art form. Crews demolished the heart of the Maxwell Street district in order to pave the way for commercial development.[2] In a time when Americans were immersed in celebrating the contributions of all Americans to the national culture, Chicago's leaders found a reason to let a cultural hearth die.

Maxwell Street fell victim to deindustrialization, a lack of urban development plans, empire building at the University of Illinois, Chicago, and the silence of the national historic preservation movement. In the face of the imminent destruction of Maxwell Street, activists in the wider preservation movement had little to say. The National Trust was quiet. The National Park Service, which administers the National Register, dismissed an application for landmark status because, in its opinion, the buildings didn't look enough like they had seventy-five years ago. The university had allowed them to deteriorate to the point where they no longer had "integrity" in the eyes of the state commission.

Of little importance at that time was the cultural continu-

Maxwell Street, Chicago, 1995
A once-vibrant neighborhood and the cultural hearth
of the electric blues, Maxwell Street fell victim to waves of urban
renewal and planned obsolescence.

ity of Maxwell Street, where blues musicians continued to perform in the street on weekends into the new century. At the very moment the university was demolishing Maxwell Street, the National Trust for Historic Preservation was giving its annual Award for Outstanding Achievement in Public Policy to Mayor

Richard Daley of Chicago, one of the prime supporters of the destruction. The decision to give Mayor Daley the preservation stamp of approval was hardly a surprise: Daley was a strong supporter of the kinds of changes that had become mainstream and that preservation leaders applauded, such as offering tax incentives to developers to preserve landmarks and rehabilitating a few highly visible historic structures like the Reliance Building, which became a luxury hotel. Preservationists eager to capitalize on one of their few sources of funding entered into a problematic marriage with developers, but in the process, perhaps unwittingly, they promoted the very policies and forces that tend to destroy the historic fabric of a city.

In praising that year's National Preservation Award winners, National Trust chief Richard Moe said, "Preservation isn't just about saving historic buildings. It's about saving historic neighborhood schools for our children, revitalizing downtowns, making historic homes affordable, and protecting our ethnic heritage." Moe had been the key figure in leading the National Trust toward a broader view of preservation, but an obvious disconnect remained between what he praised and what Mayor Daley did. Even as he helped preserve a few landmarks, Daley helped promote gentrification, pushing out not only poor and working-class people from their neighborhoods but also their legacies to the city.

The demolition of the Maxwell Street area was a crime against America's cultural memory, and it taught African Americans and all working-class people in Chicago that their history could be all too easily disposed of. If we take any solace in what happened it can be in "The Maxwell Street Teardown Blues," the farewell ode sung by Jimmie Lee Robinson before the demolition crews arrived: it became a rallying cry for those trying to preserve what was left of this and other cultural heritage sites.

The story of Maxwell Street's demise reveals the many contradictions in the way Americans have come to preserve the past since the passage of the National Historic Preservation Act.

Let me lay out some of the central problems preservationists face.

Over the course of the past hundred years the American preservation movement became largely focused on places of architectural importance, to the detriment of places of historic importance. A majority of the listings on the National Register are buildings with architectural significance. At times obsessively focused on great works of architecture, the movement has been slow to widen its scope to fight for places of cultural importance, regardless of their physical appearance. Despite some promising efforts at broadening the meaning of "preservation"—such as efforts to challenge sprawl as a threat to national historical and environmental resources—it is the Victorian house, the grand mansion, the temple of commerce that continue to dominate our national, state, and local historic registers.

This is a reversal of the goals of the movement's founding: it began more than a hundred years ago as a series of local efforts to save places of *historic* importance. The battle for Philadelphia's Independence Hall or George Washington's Mount Vernon home was waged with arguments for preserving sacred sites in the new nation's history. The 1906 Antiquities Act, the first significant piece of federal legislation, focused on Native American archaeological sites in federal parks and lands. In New York City, which pioneered many of the arguments and policies concerning preservation beginning in the early part of the twentieth century, arguments for preserving the 1812 City Hall were only tangentially about the building's elegant architectural design; what mattered were the historical events that took place there, such as the time Lincoln's body lay in state in 1865.[3]

Such initiatives, however, hardly represent a golden age of preservation to which the movement should seek to return. Preservation in the nineteenth and twentieth centuries was largely deployed as a means to "Americanize" immigrants, to commemorate the "Lost Cause" of the Confederacy in the American South, and to build places of celebratory, consensus history between white leaders of the North and South. The result was a landscape that erased and told false tales of the past in support of ongoing oppressions, of African Americans, of workers, of Native Americans. Indeed, as I'll discuss at greater length in Chapter 6, until recently American preservationists have steered away from places with controversial histories and instead sought to preserve those that would support an alleged consensus view of history, celebrating what was deemed a "shared" past (even if it was not). The result has been, as a leading preservation thinker, Ned Kaufman, has written, that they have used the notion of "heritage" to "prop up an essentially conservative ideology of cultural harmony."[4] The preservation movement is just beginning to come to terms with its own history, long after fields like history, anthropology, and urban planning began wrestling openly with their own biases and failings.

The preservation movement's hesitation to interrogate its own history and ongoing biases has meant that serious history has more often been pursued by scholars and museum personnel, where self-reflective critiques have been going on for decades. This is a shame, for something important was lost when the preservation movement prioritized architecture and ceded the telling of history to historians (and their books) and museums (and their objects). Often the most profound way to encounter—and to confront—history is in historic places.

In their focus on architectural significance, American preservationists have done little in the way of interpretation—explaining the significance of a site. The highest honor for a building—placement on the National Register of Historic Places—is commemorated by the bronze plaque affixed to it. But look closely: those plaques merely provide the name of the building and the date when it was placed on the National Register. Getting a building on the Register does not require you to explain why it's there, not even in a brochure, a webpage, or some other interpretive material. The United States does not have a system—nor does it dedicate funds—to engage writers or artists to communicate the meaning of these significant places. The place, seen as a work of art, is somehow meant to speak for itself. But as compelling as places can be to our eyes and hearts, they do not tell their stories on their own. Places do not speak; we must speak for them.

Too often in recent years, however, the way we have spoken

for old places is in the language of the market. Over the past five decades preservation of historic places has become enmeshed with the real estate market: it is now seen as a way to make money. Preservation laws and organizations emphasize the value of historic buildings for economic growth. Tax credits flow to "income-producing" properties. The market is the reference point for most American preservation-related laws and policies, and too often the greatest beneficiaries of a historic register "listing" are commercial property owners. Even if well-meaning advocates cannot create an inclusive historic district, they can secure for property owners the one tangible benefit of membership on the National Register: generous tax incentives for historic rehabilitation. The goal of preservationists has been to expand the range of places we seek to preserve. But in the United States the honors (and profits) of being "historic" flow most often into the pockets of those who own property that itself is designed to make a profit.

A further problem stems from what seems like a logical emphasis on preserving only places that can be proven to have been or to continue to be "significant." The emphasis on preserving only buildings that are visibly significant has led to bizarre cases of gerrymandering in pursuit of National Register status for historic districts.

Take New York's Lower East Side, perhaps the most famed immigrant neighborhood in the United States, which can also boast one of the most gerrymandered historic districts in the country.[5] Over the past quarter century, the Lower East Side has become hot. Tenement apartments that immigrants labored desperately to escape began selling for millions of dollars. The locus

View from the Lower East Side Tenement Museum, Orchard Street, 2013
Orchard Street and its tenements are the heart of the Lower East Side Historic
District. The Tenement Museum emphasizes the many different ethnic groups
who inhabited the neighborhood over the course of two centuries.

of the hip moved from Soho and the East Village south and east, to Rivington, Ludlow, Orchard, and Hester Streets. The inevitable followed: the neighborhood was honored as "historic" by the National Park Service, which placed the district on the National Register of Historic Places. The placement was, on one level, a victory of history over architectural elitism. Although the area does contain architecturally significant buildings, proponents of listing the district focused on its cultural importance: its role as the home of countless immigrants who arrived after 1880.

But look more closely and you'll discover that what was defined as the Lower East Side for purposes of the listing was not the entire neighborhood but rather a carefully carved section of a much larger area. The bizarre shape of this National Register district makes it look less like a coherent neighborhood and more like one of those gerrymandered voting districts, such as the snaking 12th Congressional District of North Carolina, which the Supreme Court approved on the same day the Lower East Side district received its designation in 2001. This oddly shaped plot hardly resembles the mental image current residents have of the Lower East Side, any more than it does that of those who lived here a century ago. It is a mapmaker's fiction, which reveals little about history and a lot more about the politics and practice of historic preservation in the United States.

In order to have the Lower East Side district accepted onto the revered list, advocates had to jump through the anachronistic hoops of the National Register and focus on the quality of the architecture, to reassure officials that there were enough "contributing" buildings (that is, buildings that retained most of their "original" appearance) to give a sense of what the district had looked like in the past. The inevitable result was that the advocates had to redraw the map to include buildings that helped build their case and exclude many others, regardless of their historic significance. The district was mapped to lasso in the old *Forward* newspaper building on East Broadway, the Educational Alliance Building, the Henry Street Settlement, and the Lower East Side Tenement Museum building (a previously designated National Historic Landmark). A little bump on the west side of the district is designed to incorporate the 1886 Eldridge Street Synagogue, a block beyond the Allen Street border of the actual district. At the same time, the petitioners had to leave out buildings to the east, including Saint Mary's Church (an anchor of the once strong Irish community) and Beit Hamedrash Hagadol, on Norfolk Street (once a black Baptist church and now an Orthodox Jewish synagogue), because those buildings are surrounded by modern buildings and thus could not "contribute" to the "feel" of the historic district.

The result was not a coherent historical neighborhood but a section of it. It was really a *Jewish* Lower East Side historic district—and an incomplete one at that—offered as a stand-in for the history of the entire neighborhood. It is ironic that just as the 2000 census was revealing that the United States, and New York City, were more diverse than at any time in their history, the city was creating a landmark district based largely on the past of a single group, in a neighborhood best defined as a crucible of cultures. Tour guides who led people through the Lower East Side (I was one) related the remarkable story of the various immigrant groups, living on top of one another, and more often than not in a state of harmony (or near-harmony). America's preservation rules and regulations reward cohesion when chaos, or at least vital diversity, is the exciting reality.

Many of the problems with contemporary U.S. preservation practice concern what to save, how to expand the listings, and who benefits. But a very different problem also plagues it— letting go. The preservation movement, like all of us, has a problem with death. Preservation by definition stands against the wanton destruction of the past. But by building an image of itself as a movement against destruction and in favor of keeping the past present, the preservation movement has failed to reckon with how and when to let things go.

We might go farther and say, borrowing from the philosopher Ernest Becker's 1973 study, that preservation denies death.[6] In America's system of preservation, buildings are determined to be significant for a variety of reasons. Once given recognition—on a local, state, or national register—buildings rarely are taken off the list, unless they are demolished or, in rare cases, so radically changed as to become unrecognizable. Since 1970, about 1 percent (approximately 1,800 individual sites out of a total of over 1.7 million) of "historic resources" have been removed from the National Register. Minnesota has requested removal of the most (147); Vermont has never requested that any of its sites be delisted.[7] My home state of Massachusetts, which has over 4,200 sites on the National Register (more than 5 percent of the total listings, and the second most of any state), has removed only 12 sites since 1970. And about a thousand new listings nationally are added every year.

Shouldn't Americans have a more robust process for reevaluating what they have deemed historic and for considering anew a building's importance in each generation? The Register offers virtually no guidance for reevaluating and reconsidering past decisions. So Americans are faced with ever expanding lists of important places. As Rodney Harrison has written, "We have let heritage build up on registers without thinking about what work it does in the present as an ensemble or assemblage of places." We must, he argues, "have the confidence to reconsider our heritages' histories and take the process of de-accessioning heritage seriously." Otherwise, the country will drown in ever longer lists, endless accretions of memory.[8]

The Ise Shrine in the Mie Prefecture of Japan offers a striking challenge to our usual ways of thinking, or not thinking, about death. Neither embracing preservation as Americans know it nor rejecting it, the Ise Shrine suggests a third way—preserving the design and traditional method of construction, as well as the spiritual practices taking place within sacred buildings, while allowing the buildings themselves to be torn down on a regular basis. When visitors arrive at each of the two great Shinto shrines, Naiku and Geku, they can see only the forecourts and the outlines of the main shrine beyond; few have the status to go through the gate. When I visited a few years ago, I could just see, off to the left, behind white sheets that blocked the view, the tops of bright new buildings, the wood blond in the sunlight, unlike the gray, weathered wood of the shrine in front of me. Those were part of the new temple, which was to be consecrated just a few months later, followed by the tearing down of the old one. By *old,* I mean twenty years old. Every twenty years, one shrine is torn down, and the sacred spirit and objects are moved a hundred feet to the new shrine. Each shrine is built using techniques developed a thousand years ago, and passed on to each generation. The material is new. The building is new. But the plans and the techniques are ancient. The Ise Shrine does not represent a standard approach to preservation, even in Japan. But it makes a clear

Ise Shrine, Japan, 2013
The new temple, built using centuries-old techniques, is ready to be unveiled,
twenty years after the adjacent temple was built. The "old" temple will then
be torn down, the cycle to continue.

contrast to the attitude in the United States, where the fabric of a historic building is cherished above and beyond its other values.

A radically different approach is being taken, though it continues to be debated, in Germany, at the vast landscape of the Nazi headquarters in Nuremberg, site of some of the most dramatic Party gatherings. City and national leaders decided to choose an alternative to both traditional preservation and destruction of a hateful place. To underscore and participate in the undermining of Hitler's dream of a thousand-year Reich, the city has pursued a policy of planned decay, offering interpretations of the buildings, making some safe enough to explore, but doing little to stop the impact of time and the elements. The buildings will be in hospice care for decades.[9]

These are just two examples, but they suggest that more provocative forms of acknowledging and engaging with inevitable decay are being developed and deployed far beyond the United States, though few within. Witness, for example, the debate over the World Trade Center site: initially many argued to preserve the eight-story portion of one of the twin towers that was still standing, but in the end it was removed to make way for a memorial park, a memorial museum, and office towers.[10] Americans have an allergic reaction to ruins within their midst.

In *Annie Hall,* Woody Allen declares that his philosophy of life is encapsulated in a joke about two women at a resort in the Catskills. One complains, "The food at this place is awful!" The other agrees and adds, contemptuously, "And such small portions!" That joke captures the final problem with the American way of preservation: in addition to its theoretical and practical dilemmas, preservation in the United States is also fundamentally fragile. In a country skeptical of policing private property, preservationists have little power. Buildings placed on the nation's highest list are not thereby protected from demolition. The few tools that localities have such as "demolition delays" and local historic districts provide just a faint measure of control and affect tiny portions of the country. The new places with powerful local ordinances—New York City, Boston, Savannah, and Charleston—are exceptions that because of their visibility give the impression that the preservation movement is powerful. It is not. In most of the United States, the movement is honored but frail.

Preservation differs from other forms of confronting the past because it is tied to a physical place. So the question of how the U.S. system deals with the "stuff" of place matters. The transformation of historic preservation over the course of the twentieth century from an undertaking devoted to saving historic places to a means of saving important architecture has led, almost inevitably, to a movement focused on "curatorial management of the built environment," in the words of James Marston Fitch, the founder of the first preservation program, at Columbia University.[11] In the same way museum curators would protect and carefully, scientifically, lovingly restore paintings and sculptures, preservationists would return buildings to their "original" state.

The focus within preservation on articulating the "period of significance" of a given building is inspired by the idea of curatorship. A painting or sculpture can be dated. The meaning of the work of art and the methods of restoring or preserving it are aimed at returning the work as closely as possible to its condition at the time it was created, so that viewers can experience the work as its creator intended, even as they try to find meanings that relate to the present. In the current U.S. program, deciding whether a building deserves to be listed, honored, and perhaps saved depends on when it was significant—which usually turns out to be the era in which it was created, just as with the work of art. This has the effect of wiping away the layers of subsequent history as irrelevant. I still cringe when I think of a former student who worked on the renovation of the Park Avenue Armory in New York City who was instructed to remove one beautiful layer of wallpaper after another to get back to the "original" design. One by one, each layer of history, each successive generation's aesthetic or political choice, was pulled away from the wall and thrown in the trash, in order to create a mirage of time frozen. Preservation as curatorship has at its foundation a belief in the birthdate of a work of art, and a commitment to save it, protect it, preserve it as closely as possible to its original state, so that future generations might enjoy a pure leap across time back to the artist's era.

That layers of meaning, instead, ought to be more central to historic preservation practice was brought home to me most powerfully in Rome. "History," writes the novelist Anthony Doerr, "lies beneath the city like an extensive and complicated armature. Emperors were stabbed beneath tramlines. Sheep grazed beneath supermarkets. The thirteen obelisks of Rome have been toppled and re-erected and shuffled around so many times that to lay a map of their previous positions over a map of their current ones is to evoke a miniature cross-hatching of the city's entire memory, a history of power and vanity like a labyrinth stamped beneath."[12]

The Basilica San Clemente was consecrated around 1100 and features some of Rome's finest Byzantine mosaics. There we have our "period of significance": the year the church was consecrated. But the church, like so many in Rome, was built upon earlier churches, and older sites, and it offers a two-thousand-year overview in miniature of Rome's history and architecture. The basilica's layers have been steadily excavated since the mid-nineteenth century. Passing through the gorgeous "new" basilica of the 1100s, visitors can now descend through the layers to the fourth-century basilica, and then to the first-century Roman buildings (which include a mithraeum, a sacred space below ground for the practitioners of the religion of Mithraism), and, below that, the remains of a building destroyed by the great fire of 64 C.E. When you reach this level, in the winding passageways of the excavations, you can hear the sound of rushing water, and soon you come across the clear spring that was in this place long before any of the ancient layers of the basilica, and which called to people to build the first homes here. Discovering this ancient and persistent stream, thirty feet below the current street level, was a stunning experience; I have heard the rushing waters of San Clemente in my head on numerous occasions since I visited.

A short walk from San Clemente is the Roman Forum, the most visited site, along with the adjacent Colosseum, in the ancient city. Since ruins are commonly equated with the "authentic," visitors walking through acres of ruins testifying to the storybook images of Caesar, the Roman Senate, and the fall of Rome, might believe they have arrived at the untouched remains of the Roman Empire, its civic and commercial core, the Forum Romanum. I certainly thought so when in 1984 I made my way down a long ramp from the via dei Fori Imperiali into the ruins, sacred grounds of Western civilization. What I didn't know then, and had not been taught, was that this was an urban renewal zone, where nineteenth- and twentieth-century archaeologists and political leaders, among them Mussolini, removed more than a millennium's worth of post-imperial human settlement in order to feed their longing for a mythical Roman past or, as in Mussolini's case, to buttress claims to be a modern Caesar. Sacred ground for classicists, it is a crime scene for those who would tell the story of medieval Rome. The wholesale destruction has led some people to despise the place.

Rome can teach the lesson particularly well that where people have lived for generations, layers are added, and all those layers should be at the core of what we celebrate when we preserve and reuse a place for a new generation. The "idol of origins," attacked by the historian Marc Bloch in his critique of historical writing, leads those in the field of preservation to want to scrape away history and return to a pristine moment of creation, as if no one ever lived in the designated house—never made a mess, added an ugly lamp, removed the front porch, or put in the latest, most fashionable wallpaper, which was then removed by the next owner.[13] This craving for the most significant moment in the history of a place ultimately came to be cemented into America's preservation culture and program. But at last it is being displaced.

Across the United States, historic sites are starting to denounce the "idol of origins" and celebrate the range of people over time who have lived in a place. The Lower East Side Tenement Museum organizes its story of 97 Orchard Street not around 1863, when the building was built, but around a series of rooms that show how different families lived there over the course of a century. At Monticello, historians and descendants of slaves have pushed to present the significance of one of the nation's most cherished historical sites as not only the story of Thomas Jefferson but also that of Sally Hemings, through interpretation of both the mansion and Mulberry Row, the main street of the plantation.

The nation's preservation regulations are catching up as well. Under pressure from advocates hoping to broaden the definition of "significance," the National Park Service has issued a series of bulletins encouraging new types of places to be nominated to the Register, places that do not fit the mold of the beautiful building. "Traditional cultural properties" are places whose "significance derived from the role the property plays in a community's historically rooted beliefs, customs, and practices."[14] They have especially been focused on Native American sites but also include places such as Bohemian Hall in Queens, New York, a longstanding Czech and Slovak cultural center and beer garden.[15] These changes have taken place because of pressure from activists demanding that Americans honor the range of places and their stories that make up an increasingly kaleidoscopic citizenry.

The process is slow and requires in many situations rethinking the stories places tell, trying to return the layers of history that have been scraped away with jackhammers, or in words spoken or left out.

The truth is, preservationists should be using virtually every site to highlight the physical story but also the imaginative ones that accrued in a place over successive generations. Such messiness lies at the root of the power of place—a power that allows us, if we preserve and interpret well, to imagine the act of settlement, the laying out of a plot of land, planning what to build, constructing a place, and then seeing, with equal clarity, in words and in space, how people lived there, one generation to the next.

4 preservation and economic justice

I attended the annual meeting of the National Trust for Historic Preservation in Savannah, Georgia, in the fall of 2014. During one time slot I found myself interested in two sessions, located in adjacent rooms. I walked into the first room, and it was packed with about two hundred preservationists. Donovan Rypkema, the leading figure in the effort to quantify the economic value of historic preservation to cities and states, was speaking. He began, somewhat defensively, by stating what he has said several times in print: "The educational, cultural, aesthetic, social, and historical values of historic preservation are more important than the economic value."[1] People nodded. And then Rypkema launched into his presentation, which was entirely concerned with the varied ways preservation makes good economic sense. I moved next door to the other session—three presentations on "sites of conscience," including one by Rob Nieweg, the National Trust field staff person who has been supporting the efforts of Ana Edwards and the Sacred Ground Coalition in Richmond's Shockoe Bottom to save, interpret, and memorialize the place where slaves were bought, sold, imprisoned, and buried. Although it was being held in a ballroom as big as the neighboring session's room, this panel had attracted about twenty people. And two hundred to twenty is just about the proportion of energy focused within the American preservation world on preservation for economic development versus preservation for other values. No matter how often people insist that economics is not the primary reason for preserving the past, the evidence within the profession suggests otherwise.

Preservation and real estate development have come to be inseparable. Little preservation work seems to take place outside the market, and the most important determinant of whether a building will be saved is whether there is a profit to be made. In preservationists' efforts to become central to economic development and planning discussions, have they become overly reliant on tax and other market incentives as drivers of preservation programs? Have they been too satisfied with increasing property values and generating more local taxes, and not paid enough attention to the problems of inequality and economic dislocation? Are advocates for preservation as a means of economic development in effect following the trickle-down theory: Do whatever it takes to attract rich people back to the cities and restore the buildings and that will increase tax receipts, and all will be well?

The story of two houses in two American cities helps explain the dilemma.

FOR SALE, $20,000: 1196 HADDON
AVENUE, CAMDEN, NEW JERSEY

The trip on the High Speed train line from Locust Street in Center City, Philadelphia, to Camden's City Hall stop takes about eight minutes. But the distance is from two ends of the economic spectrum and two ends of America's urban situation. It is the distance between bustling, revitalized downtown Philadelphia, a symbol of the rejuvenation of U.S. cities in the past quarter century, and the desolation of Camden, one of the most impoverished cities in America. Drive through Camden for an hour and you will see devastation on a monumental scale, a situation that is replicated in old industrial cities across the country.

My mother grew up in Camden, first on Kaighn Avenue, and then at 1196 Haddon Avenue in the then predominantly Jewish neighborhood of Parkside. My grandfather had a kosher butcher store. My aunt and uncle had a lamp store down the street. Camden was a busy city of industry and immigrants, home of Campbell's Soup, RCA, a navy yard. Jewish and Italian immigrants made homes here and found good work.

Immigrants from Europe were followed by black migrants from the South. While my mother's yearbook had a smattering of black faces, once those faces reached what was seen as a "tipping point," the white people—my family included—started moving out.

1196 Haddon Avenue, Camden, New Jersey, 2011
My mother's French Second Empire–inspired row house, with the family
kosher butcher on the first floor, sits empty and boarded up in one of the
poorest cities in the United States.

The lamp store moved just beyond Camden to a mini-mall along
the new Route 73; Aunt Hilda and Uncle Joe moved themselves
to Cherry Hill. The rest of the family soon followed them to the
suburbs. In the process many also moved from union membership at Campbell's or RCA and into business ownership and more
conservative politics. This is a story that Americans know too well:
deindustrialization, disinvestment, racist policies, economic apartheid, municipal corruption, and the conservative revolt.

I was drawn to Camden as a young man attending the University of Pennsylvania, where I studied urban history, and I took several drives into the city with my uncle Joe. It is easy to avoid Camden. The interstate highways were built in part to allow cars to bypass the places they and their businesses had fled. My relatives, all born and bred in Camden, relocated to the suburban fringes and never went back. My mother's fiftieth high school reunion was held in a restaurant—in Cherry Hill. Not a soul went back to Camden High.

My relatives were dismayed that I would exit off Admiral Wilson Boulevard and drive through the city streets. Once I noticed that the house and kosher butcher shop on Haddon Avenue, which on other visits had been boarded up, had a new for-sale sign. I wrote down the phone number and kept it. A year later, after Uncle Joe died, I convinced my elegant aunt Hilda, the inspiration behind the lamp designs at her store that populated living rooms in southern New Jersey through the 1990s, to visit it with me. The owner, thinking we might buy it for nostalgia's sake, unscrewed the boards covering the entrance, and we peered in at a complete ruin. It was impossible to imagine the butcher store I had seen in old family photos. We thought of walking in—until the owner took one step and fell three feet down to the subfloor.

Today a halal butcher stands across the street, which makes for an ironic—and even hopeful—twist in a neighborhood once filled with Jewish immigrants. In the intervening generations, mainly black families have struggled to keep the buildings from falling down. But without jobs or public investment this neighborhood is a shell of its former self, with little hope for the future.

Preservation is part of Philadelphia's past and future. We

could debate endlessly the impact of gentrification on Philadelphia's Center City neighborhoods, and I would argue that in north Philadelphia, which lost a hundred thousand jobs and its industrial base in the 1970s and 1980s, the devastation comes close to that of Camden. Nonetheless, there is no doubt that the economic vitality of Philadelphia's Center City downtown is in significant measure due to the attraction of the old homes and neighborhoods to those who can afford them.

But if you cross the Ben Franklin Bridge and park in front of 1196 Haddon Avenue, you might wonder what historic preservation has to offer it. Making a case for the mansard roof and Queen Anne detailing on the second-floor bay windows, narrating the rich history of the neighborhood, seem not only inadequate to the crisis here but dismissive of it. To talk about tax incentives that might help a storeowner repair a facade seems ludicrous. To encourage "main street" improvements—red-brick sidewalks, street lamps—to attract business is like offering a band-aid for an amputated limb. The language and the tools of preservation appear to have little to give one of America's most glaring exemplars of inequality—the desolate inner city. A progressive preservation movement will justify itself only when it has something tangible to offer places like Camden.

FOR SALE, $3.5 MILLION: 555 HUDSON STREET, WEST VILLAGE, NEW YORK

I followed the lure of a real estate advertisement. The three-story building at 555 Hudson Street was for sale in 2009 for a cool $3.5 million. I went to see it, expecting on the one hand to

The corner of Hudson Street, seen from inside 555 Hudson Street, 2009
Upscale coffee shops like Le Pain Quotidien are common in this gentrified
neighborhood, where the urbanist Jane Jacobs once led the crusade to save
mixed-use, diversely populated districts.

make a spiritual connection to its former owner, the urbanist and writer Jane Jacobs, author of *The Death and Life of Great American Cities,* as if, forty years after she left the house, nothing would have changed. But I also went to see what she had seen, to look out at the street from her living-room window. High expectations were met by deep disappointment. It was, of course, nothing more than a decent, somewhat rickety, narrow house with a first-floor retail space, an open living-room area on the second floor, a small kitchen, tiny bedrooms, a lovely third-floor patio, and a dark backyard (with a fence memorably captured by Diane Arbus when she photographed Jacobs and her son Ned). Temporary furniture had been placed in the rooms by the real estate company to help sell the house.

It is impossible not to appreciate what Jane Jacobs achieved here. As an organizer she helped stop the neighborhood's demolition to make way for an onramp of the Lower Manhattan Expressway, a Robert Moses project. And in celebrating the vitality that a mixture of people and activities gave to a city, she helped bring people back to appreciate what cities could offer that suburbs and small towns could not.

But even as my admiration for Jane Jacobs soared once again, that $3.5 million price tag gnawed. Jacobs fought alongside others in the early 1960s to save the West Village from destruction and won an important victory that would ultimately bring down the urban renewal edifice. But even as she saved the neighborhood, she failed to reckon with what it might become: an enclave for the wealthy. On the outside, everything has been preserved—a remarkable victory against yet another highway project. But behind the facades, the neighborhood has been transformed by a postindustrial globalized economy that has re-sorted New York, clearing lower Manhattan of the working classes and repopulating it with the super-rich. Without intending it, but perhaps without being able to anticipate it, Jacobs had made the neighborhood safe for $3.5 million townhouses.

Given her prescience and her ability to articulate principles of city building that are widely employed today, Jacobs missed one fundamental calculation. She loved old buildings because she felt they would be cheaper than newer buildings and therefore working people, artists and musicians, and new kinds of businesses would be encouraged to buy them. What she failed to incorporate into her theory of urban revitalization was that old buildings would become the most valuable properties in many urban districts. In Greenwich Village today, millionaires gravitate not to the newer buildings but to brick and brownstone row houses. Jacobs did not anticipate the economy that was just beginning to develop, but she would play a part in it—she, a journalist and writer, and her husband, an architect, were in the vanguard of young professionals who created an economic model that would remake the city.

In Jacobs's theory, older buildings put a damper on the overheating real estate market; with their relatively low rents, they kept neighborhoods economically diverse and eased their growth and transition as new buildings were erected. The opposite turned out to be the case. When Jacobs looked out her window in the late 1950s she could see, across the street, Joe Carnacchio, son of Italian immigrants, in his butcher store. When I looked out that same window a half century later I saw a Pain Quotidien, an upscale chain where a cup of coffee and muffin could be had for a mere ten dollars. Jacobs saw the world built by postwar American economic and political might, a world where even in New York decent working-class jobs could be found, strong unions flourished, and municipal governments kept subways running, built public housing, and invested in public schools. Jacobs could reasonably celebrate the workings of the real estate market and suggest that small-scale capitalism functioned like an ecosystem because she assumed that investments and regulations would help maintain her neighborhood. New York's economy, its labor unions, and federal, state, and local investments were supporting a broad middle class. When I looked out her window in the new millennium, New York was a different place. The buildings were the same—and that is good for architectural historians as well as citizens, and the environment—but the economic situation of the people living in them, and therefore of the stores and businesses around them, was different. This is a Potemkin village, a beautiful neighborhood that looks like a Jacobs ideal, except for the most fundamental part, the dense mix of people and incomes.

In the United States, when it comes to urban economic development and equity, historic preservation gets three raps, from three different constituencies.

The left accuses the historic preservation movement of facilitating gentrification, whereby working people are pushed out of their old neighborhoods by rich newcomers eager for urban life. By saving old buildings and cherishing them, so the argument goes, preservationists have enticed rich people back to the city, where they colonize neighborhoods they or their parents or grandparents left long ago and drive the prices up out of the reach of the current residents. When apartments started selling for a million dollars on Orchard Street in the Lower East Side of New York City, across from the Tenement Museum, it was proof that preservationists had succeeded beyond their wildest dreams—or failed beyond their worst nightmares.

The right, on the other hand, accuses the preservation movement of preventing new housing from being built, and of stunting needed growth. Even as preservationists are charged with forcing the working classes out to distant parts of the city or suburbs, they are attacked for impeding the free market in real estate by unnaturally preventing developers from tearing down three-story row houses and building ten-story apartment buildings in their place, all of which, free marketers argue, would stimulate the economy and lower housing prices. Thus, in part because of excessive preservation, they say, American cities face a housing shortage.

Where the right and left agree is in accusing the preservation movement of being elitist and irrelevant to the pressing, desperate needs of urban areas, as well as the problems faced in small towns and rural areas. Insisting that a WalMart have a mansard roof "to make it fit in" while ignoring its devastating economic impact on small town centers convinces many critics that preservationists have little to contribute to progressive economic development.

Unfortunately, there is some truth to each of these accusations.

But there need not be. Preservation does not have to be paired with gentrification, or absent from the poorest areas, or a contributor to the housing crisis. It can, in fact, be a tool for securing more just communities. If preservationists truly care about creating dense cities and towns without pushing out the poor, they will have to offer a new model for saving both buildings and communities. Preservation has to be reconfigured as a social justice movement or else it will have lost its moral compass. Politics inheres in every choice humans make about what to preserve and how to preserve it. The historic preservation movement must be reconfigured as a key ally in a broader movement for social justice.

HISTORIC PRESERVATION PAYS

Historic preservation pays. Numerous studies show that investment by cities and states in preserving and restoring old places produces new construction jobs, business development, tourism, and increased tax dollars.[2] This is the one area of historic preservation that has been well studied, with dozens of detailed analyses of the value of preservation for generating economic activity. Preservationists, following the zeitgeist whereby value equates to economic gain, have spent a great deal of energy promoting the idea that preservation is good for economic development and tax revenues. Although in what follows I focus on the U.S. situation, preservationists worldwide are making similar economic arguments.

The arguments and proof are now well established: state investment (via federal and state tax credits or direct grants) spurs a range of private investment. Investment in old buildings is more likely to support local craftspeople and small businesses and generate more local economic activity. New construction, by contrast, is more likely to take the form of big-box multinational chain stores. Furthermore, investment in historic areas has been shown to be more lasting, creating local construction jobs and spurring the establishment of small businesses in traditional storefronts, which typically remain in business longer than stores in malls or other new commercial areas. Historic preservation also promotes more visits (and spending) from regional customers, while at the same time encouraging heritage tourism, especially drawing international travelers who will, if they visit, stay longer and spend more money. Historic preservation, by spurring investment by businesses and encouraging the wealthy to buy previously vacated or underutilized buildings in town and city centers, increases property values, thereby increasing tax revenues in an era when taxes have typically stagnated or gone down. Preservationists will argue that few other economic investments produce as much economic activity, over a longer period, and in a wider range of the economy for so little initial investment.

Developers and business owners have not gotten the word, however, or still don't believe it. Many businesspeople believe that preservationists' favorite word is *no.* Much of the criticism concerns the regulatory hurdles preservationists put in the way, whether in enabling a business to qualify for tax credits or in allowing it to make changes to a building in a historic district.

Business owners using or planning to use historic buildings for their businesses or residential developments typically say that preservationists are interested in "stasis" or "preserving buildings in amber" and that locating a business in a historic building usually means "obstacles." In Holyoke, Massachusetts, for example, developers eager to take over some of the long-vacant mill buildings have balked at applying for tax credits because they doubt that doing so will make economic sense owing to all the strictures involved in meeting rehabilitation standards set by the secretary of the interior and in being evaluated by the local historical commission.[3]

Criticisms of the alignment of preservation with economic development focus on tax credits, which became a central source of support for U.S. preservation programs beginning in the decade or two after the ratification of the National Historic Preservation Act. The 1976 Tax Reform Act was the most important new legislation; it established substantial federal income tax incentives for preservation projects. The 1981 Economic Recovery Tax Act expanded the incentives and focused on income-producing properties. For many, the potential of the NHPA was only realized when tax credits were established, for now preservation for aesthetic or historic reasons had become profitable and thus "realistic."

The relentless focus in the United States on tax credits has had a substantial downside. In spending so much energy protecting, expanding, and using tax credits to save historic buildings the movement deemphasizes some of its core values—trying to save the places that are the most significant and most meaningful to a town or region and its inhabitants. Advocates making the argument for the economic value of historic preservation fawn over the numbers showing the value of federal and state tax credits. But preservation by tax credit quickly moves the field away from its core mission of figuring out, in Tom Mayes's words, which old places matter. It is preservation in reverse—if a developer is interested, preservationists will help prove that the property qualifies for a tax credit. The development–tax credit approach steers preservation work away from homes, and away from poorer areas. City leaders and preservation advocates put most of their efforts into commercial projects, and not into preserving other places of significance. They follow the money.

Meanwhile, people on the right pinpoint preservation as a principal cause of the shortage of affordable urban housing. Preservation has, goes the argument, effectively limited developers' ability to build more housing and thus made it harder for the poor who have been displaced by gentrification to find new homes within the city. Pandering to the wealthy and forcing out the working class—preservationists are accused of causing both problems.

The tension between the values of preservation and those of greater density and affordable housing in cities was forcefully articulated by the Harvard economist Edward Glaeser in a widely discussed book, *Triumph of the City.* Glaeser's head-on attack on historic preservation in the United States claimed that it undermined the necessary development and redevelopment of cities; as he argued, one of the causes of the high price of real estate in New York was the limitation on building size and density mandated by the city's Landmarks Preservation Commission and its historic districts. Glaeser charged that preservation effectively halted the market-driven redevelopment of older districts to make buildings taller and thus more densely populated, which would create more affordable housing as well as greener cities (buildings that are close together use less heat). Glaeser posed what he called "the real question": "whether these vast districts should ever have been created and whether they should remain protected ground in the years ahead." His answer: "No living city's future should become a prisoner to its past."[4]

Preservationists roared in fury, and with good reason. It is preposterous, as many have pointed out, to claim that preservation restrictions, which cover only a small portion of the housing stock in New York City, could prevent the growth of affordable housing. Furthermore, most new building is in the luxury sector, as exemplified by massive coops such as 15 Central Park West—or the most expensive of all residential towers at its completion, 432 Park Avenue, a building that represented, for the *New Yorker* columnist Adam Gopnik, the "things that give cities a bad conscience." The Park Avenue building, he suggested, "the tallest, ugliest, and among the most expensive private residences in the city's history—the Oligarch's Erection, as it should be known," served as "a catchment for the rich from which to look down on everyone else . . . it is hard not to feel that the civic virtues of commonality have been betrayed." None of these buildings, all of which have the low density of country-club suburbs, with a family of four living on two or three floors, contributes to expanding the stock of affordable housing.[5]

It is wrong to blame the preservation movement for the lack of affordable housing when the real estate industry, supported by city administrations, seems focused on luxury housing. But the fallacy in Glaeser's argument goes deeper. The market cannot be relied on to bring in needed investment, and to make it in an equitable way. The market, far from being a color-blind system of allocating investment dollars, operates within a legacy of racism, segregation, and economic inequality. And preservationists need to address this issue. As one advocate, Andrew Hurley, writes, "To reassert its relevance as a tool for revitalization the preservation movement must find ways to accommodate and reward a wider range of heritage-based revitalization strategies."[6]

As I discussed earlier, with a few exceptions, U.S. preservation laws are remarkably weak. In most communities, preservation is little more than a work of valorization, not regulation. Only in a few places—which get a lot of press because they are big cities: San Francisco, New York, Boston—do preservation regulations have the power to stop buildings from being altered or destroyed. In the heat of a battle around an individual project, those in favor decry the "stranglehold" preservation has on new development. They are almost always wrong. That argument is a straw man, and preservationists have rightly called it so. And they have been right to claim victimhood, as the David against Goliath, wielding only a slingshot of regulatory powers against the real estate development giant.

The National Trust's Preservation Green Lab has produced a report designed to rebut Glaeser. In *Older, Smaller, Better* the authors argue that simply building more densely does not make cities better. In fact, the most vibrant cities are more like the city Jane Jacobs promoted in the early 1960s: "Established neighborhoods with a mix of older, smaller buildings perform better than districts with larger, newer structures when tested against a range of economic, social, and environmental outcome measures."[7] Preservation of historic districts does not impede density and the creation of affordable housing, but it does maintain scale and cultural values that draw people and business. Glaeser leaves out of his argument the unintended consequences of turning the city over to developers, consequences that are highlighted in the Green Lab report. Glaeser's analysis also fails to account for other, less tangible factors that will make a city both attractive and viable as an economic engine. And by focusing on New York, Glaeser limits the scope of his argument: the notion that preservationists are inhibiting the creation of affordable housing in Baltimore or Detroit, both with vast stretches of vacant buildings and land, is ridiculous. In much of the country, preservation is a tool for the creation of new housing, and helps prevent the mass demolition that is the favored, but flawed, policy of many cities.

GENTRIFICATION

Of all the debates over the relationship between preservation and economic development, the most contentious centers around gentrification. The *Oxford English Dictionary*'s definition of *gentrification* is simply "the process by which an (urban) area is rendered middle-class" (or upper class). That process involves a migration of wealthier people into an area of mainly lower-income people—or at least, lower-income than the migrants. It is usually accompanied by new buildings or rehabilitation of older buildings, with new, more expensive stores following right behind the high-income residents.

The case against gentrification has become a standard in urban development debates. Gentrification leads to raised rents and the displacement of long-time residents. Landlords find they can raise their rents, steadily pushing out long-time tenants and neighborhood stores. The result is that not only do long-time residents have to find new homes, but the identity of the neighborhood is transformed, and rapidly, by what the writer Michael Sorkin calls the "cruel cleansing of gentrification." Just as my mother's neighborhood could "flip" as white ethnics fled in the face of what they perceived of as an "invasion" by African Americans, so now those same white ethnics—older Italian or Irish Americans—must find new homes as "yuppies" (in the 1980s terminology) move in. The identity shift is often symbolized through neighborhood name changes—Bushwick (a long troubled neighborhood) is now called East Williamsburg; Spanish Harlem has been turned into "SpaHa." The resentment at the effect of gentrification in transforming the character of a neighborhood can be powerful.[8]

Historic buildings are, as Tom Mayes argued, central to creating and maintaining our identity as individuals and communities. So the rapid transformation of a neighborhood, even if the buildings remain the same, can be destabilizing. Old buildings have been the silent partners in gentrification—buildings long ignored suddenly find admirers with money circling like bees to honey. Preservationists, by encouraging redevelopment of historic buildings and harnessing tax credits with greater energy, have at times been forces for displacement and encouraging the segregation of cities by class. The historian Suleiman Osman, who grew up as Brooklyn was gentrifying, notes that preservation itself suffers when it seems to be "striking a Faustian bargain with developers."[9]

To be fair, the impact of gentrification is more complicated than critiques about invading yuppies and slippery bankers have allowed. Wealthy white homeowners have often helped rehabilitate buildings, develop commercial areas, and build coalitions of long-time residents to fight redlining (the practice by which banks refuse to invest in poorer and minority neighborhoods). And because of the influence of the new residents, the neighborhood often sees new investment in schools and public spaces. Some in-migrants (a less loaded term) show interest, as Osman has shown, in fighting off urban renewal while defending rent control and the rights of minority residents. The sociologist Japonica Brown-Saracino has similarly tried to rescue the image of "gentrifiers" from the clichés of the rapacious investor or the rich suburbanite interested in a more "authentic" home. She finds that some gentrifiers hope to become involved in neighborhood revitalization that benefits everyone. These "social preservationists" have a more sophisticated understanding of preservation's role in transforming neighborhoods and seek to be active in combating the destruction of their neighborhood's social and economic basis.[10]

Others have complicated one of the central criticisms of

gentrification—that it promotes displacement of long-time residents. In *There Goes the 'Hood,* Lance Freeman, a professor of urban planning at Columbia University, studied two gentrifying neighborhoods—Clinton Hill in Brooklyn and Harlem (where he lives) in Manhattan—expecting to find fairly substantial displacement and dissatisfaction in each. He uncovered, to his surprise, little correlation between gentrification and neighborhood displacement. In fact, he discovered in these two neighborhoods that more people were losing their homes because of physical collapse than from being forced out by rising rents. And those who left often found better housing conditions elsewhere.[11]

Finally, pro-gentrification writers argue that although there may be places where the transformation of a neighborhood's demographics is rapid, these are in the minority. Most neighborhoods desperately need more investment, and gentrification brings with it some major benefits for residents who stay: lower crime rates, better policing, more and better selection in shops, and so on. As Freeman writes, "The discourse on gentrification has tended to overlook the possibility that some of the neighborhood changes associated with gentrification might be appreciated by the prior residents." Andrew Hurley, who has fought for using preservation and public history as tools in the equitable redevelopment of North Saint Louis, argues that the movement has not employed the greater range of tools that could help in the renovation of working-class districts. American cities need more investment in poorer neighborhoods, not less. "We need gentrification," says Brad White, a long-time preservation advocate who was appointed by President Barack Obama to the Advisory

Council on Historic Preservation. "We need investment." *New York* magazine put the matter bluntly in a review of Freeman's book: "The ailing cities that save themselves in the 21st century will do so by following Brooklyn's blueprint. They'll gentrify as fast as they can."[12] Supporters of preservation as a means of economic development have argued that by becoming a part of the real estate development world preservation has finally become central to city planning and economic development, without losing the essential goal of saving from destruction important historic sites.

While valuable for complicating the story about who is gentrifying and where, and how great gentrification's negative impact might be, some of these writers may have missed the forest for the trees. When we peer down from a higher vantage point, American cities, and to greater and lesser degrees cities around the world, have been subject to a dramatic resorting. Many gentrifiers, backed by city development policies, took over low-rent rooming houses, worked against public housing, and strategically displaced low-income residents. Gentrification, a term that came into common use only in the 1980s, dates back to a more fundamental shift in the economy of America's large cities, away from manufacturing and toward a more divided service economy, which brought enormous upheaval to working-class and minority communities. Gentrification, with historic preservation playing a supporting role, has aided that destabilizing transformation.

But what should be of greater concern than evaluating the preservation movement's culpability or innocence in the problems faced by poor and minority residents is that virtually no one fundamentally challenges the idea that markets can produce more egalitarian cities. With a little tweaking here and there, the mantra remains "Let the market do its work." In a neoliberal model, where the free market reigns, the "best" thing for a neighborhood is for rich people to buy property, fix it up, bring in more people, and build new stores and businesses. Gentrifiers see this as the way to improve districts. City officials follow the logic and hope to lure rich people by encouraging reuse of old mills as condominiums, fixing up downtown districts to make them more appealing to artists, and the like. Neighborhood activists may acknowledge the advantages of increased police presence, new supermarkets, and investment in parks, but they decry the fact that it took the influx of wealthy (and usually white) people, the displacement of long-time residents, and a tangible change in the character of the community to bring about such improvements, for which they had long advocated.

In the face of the problems caused by gentrification, for example, activists have offered few coherent responses. They might organize boycotts of new coffee shops in formerly working-class neighborhoods, as in the Pilsen neighborhood of Chicago or Boyle Heights in Los Angeles. Or they might indulge in personal flareups, as was dramatized in the confrontation between the young men in Bedford-Stuyvesant and a white yuppie in Spike Lee's *Do the Right Thing* (1988), one of the most powerful portrayals of the politics of gentrification and the clash of races. In the movie, an accidental, but unacknowledged, scuffing of his brand-new Air Jordans leads Buggin' Out, a young black man from the neighborhood, to confront Clifton, a white man wearing a Celtics basketball jersey and carrying a carton of Tropicana orange juice. After seeking an apology for the scuffed shoes, Buggin' Out asks, "What you want to live in a black neighborhood for anyway, man?" adding "Motherfuck gentrification" for good measure. (Why Clifton wanted to live there seems obvious to most viewers: to take advantage of beautiful, affordable brownstones on a quiet block.)

But that such responses—stopping Starbucks, shunning the boutique, protesting the young professional or artist who has moved into the neighborhood and is renovating a previously dilapidated building—have come to stand for political action and a theory of development reveals the poverty of our economic development strategies, many of which seem like scraps from the neoliberal table. Americans promote gentrification as a tool of economic development, but they do not address the concomitant social issues. Even in New York, under a reasonably progressive mayor like Bill de Blasio, the city's tools are limited—the best that preservationists seem able to do is promote more market-driven development with some controls, so that gentrification is slowed. Despite some hopeful signs, such as the passage of inclusionary zoning rules and requiring affordable housing to be built as part of market-rate developments, the city's economic development policy still involves luring wealthy people—what the urban theorist Richard Florida calls the "creative class"—back to cities.[13] And preservation has become, in part by the movement's own design and in part by being coopted by the market, a central tool in their transformation.

The fundamental failure in the "preservation as economic development" model is that it looks to economic growth and activity and not to economic equity or economic justice. In the United States, "economic development" has grown tremendously in the past twenty years. But virtually all of it went to people in the top 1 percent of income. While there is much evidence that preservation projects take place in a wide range of neighborhoods, the predominant argument for preservation as a form of economic development still focuses on tax receipts, businesses, and investment. A robust preservation real estate market, so the argument goes, will generate economic growth beneficial to all. It rarely does. Why must for-profit development of property be at the center of community transformation? Why do Americans accept that dominance of the market? They don't have to. As Hurley has written: "Left alone, market-driven historic preservation in inner-city districts invariably results in some destructive displacement. But the process does not have to be left alone."[14]

Preservationists need to develop new forms of ownership—or revive older forms of public ownership—in order to rein in the inequities of the market; they must adopt new forms of advocacy that aim not just for economically vibrant communities, but economically just ones. If preservationists care about creating dense cities and towns but reject the re-sorting by class that often results from gentrifying historic districts, they will have to offer a new model for saving buildings and communities. This means, for example, embracing—or re-embracing—public housing and rent control. As Sorkin has argued, Americans need to look far-ther back than the 1965 law creating the Landmarks Preservation Commission. "New York's most important piece of preservation legislation," he argues, "was passed in 1942: our rent regulations." Rent regulations, while having little to do with architectural preservation, nonetheless serve the values of a progressive preser-vation movement. They are "bulwarks of community, cementing diversity and thwarting destruction of human habitat: these laws landmark lives. Our architectural landmark laws don't." Preser-vationists need, Sorkin suggests, to "link architectural preser-vation to human preservation," acting on the analogy between goals of architectural preservation and goals for citizens, "princi-pally the right to remain, itself an enshrined human right."[15]

But preservationists across America must also embrace new forms of property ownership, like community land trusts and mutual housing, as a way to protect against the shifting tides of private investment. They must pass ordinances such as those I noted earlier in San Francisco, which provide financial sup-port to help communities save not only their buildings but also businesses that, by virtue of their longevity, have become part of neighborhood identity. They must promote the kind of work Historic Boston does to restore dilapidated structures for af-fordable housing—such as Kittredge House in Roxbury—as the basis for neighborhood economic development. They need to join the kind of grassroots housing and cultural projects in the context of real community empowerment pioneered in Houston's Project Row Houses and Chicago's South Side Rebuild Founda-tion's Dorchester Projects.[16]

The time has come to return the "movement" to the American preservation movement by taking to the streets in alliance with other organizations to protest displacement and disinvestment where it is happening. The activists with Boston's City Life/La Vida Urbana may not call themselves preservationists. But when they form a line across a sidewalk, risking arrest, so that a sheriff cannot evict a tenant under proceedings based on the owner's mortgage foreclosure by a large bank or block the doorway of City Hall to protest eviction notices, they are performing an act of preservation, not only of an individual's home, but of the community in which the tenant lived. Graciela Isabel Sánchez, an activist with the Esperanza Peace and Justice Center in San Antonio, argues that "preservationists must become anti-gentrification activists. . . . If historic preservationists are serious about the desire to preserve the history and culture of communities of color, they must find ways to prevent the gentrification of inner-city communities."[17] Traditional preservation organizations should stand with these groups and activists. There are legions of preservationists who have stood at the barricades—or, rather, in front of bulldozers—to protect a cherished historic building. But their stories seem to be found mainly in black-and-white photographs. The American preservation movement has traded social protest for a place at the table of mainstream economic development strategies. The question deserves to be asked: For what are preservationists prepared to be arrested?

Inspiration for new models requires Americans to look far beyond their own borders. Berlin's International Building Exhibition (IBA) of the 1980s, one of the most important housing and

International Building Exhibition, Berlin, 2011
IBA combined new architecture (at right and left) with the old to "critically reconstruct" the city. Most of the buildings in the decade-long project in the 1980s were low- and middle-income housing.

city planning initiatives of the twentieth century (unfortunately largely ignored, in part because the Berlin Wall fell just as the project reached completion), sponsored architectural competitions and then financed hundreds of building projects, pioneered the "critical reconstruction" of West Berlin using historic preservation principles, and maintained throughout an unyielding focus on affordable and middle-class housing in the still war-ravaged parts of the city.

IBA brought world-famous architects to Berlin, but insisted

that they tame their egos to meet the needs of the city. Architects John Hejduk, Aldo Rossi, Rob Krier, and Daniel Libeskind were all forced to modify their designs to fit IBA's overall scheme for reconstructing the cityscape. IBA planned and built gardens and parks, a power station, a scientific research center, schools, day-care centers, and retail space. But mainly IBA built thousands of new units of low-income housing and renovated upward of ten thousand units in the city's impoverished industrial district of Kreuzberg. IBA-Alt—the division dedicated to rehabilitation—was more radical than its IBA-Neu new-construction counter-part. Led by the architect and urban planner Hardt-Waltherr Hämer, IBA-Alt supported squatters who had taken over empty buildings from absent landlords and speculators, insisting on democratic participation of residents in all projects, and encour-aging residents' help in construction in order to keep rents low.

Hampered by the Berlin Wall, and by its own approach of doing "careful urban renewal," IBA became, perhaps unwillingly and unwittingly, one of the most humble and yet far-reaching urban rehabilitation projects of the past century. It brought good design and historic rehabilitation—rarely aesthetically inspired but usually very appealing—to devastated regions of the city. Urbanism trumped architecture, and preservation stood on equal footing with new building by young "starchitects."

For inspiration, American preservationists should also look south, to Cuba, especially now that after a half century the United States and its island enemy are heading toward regular relations, including lifting the embargo on travel. Like President Barack Obama, thousands of Americans each year will visit Havana and enjoy the fruits of a remarkable preservation effort in the Old City. In Havana, the most important figure in economic development is the city historian. For many years the post was held by Eusebio Leal, who convinced Cuba's leaders Fidel and Raúl Castro that they could use history to milk hard currency from foreign visitors while also beautifying the city and doing it in a way that would honor their political principles. The Office of the City Historian effectively owns all of historic Havana. It has welcomed tourists (for their hard currency) and allowed hotels and restaurants to be established, producing income for the city and nation. But the office has not turned Old Havana into a Disneyland. Instead, the historians proceeded with two principles in mind. First, although they would renovate ground floors for tourist-oriented businesses, they would retain regular housing on the upper stories. Walking through Havana, you can see, at eye level, cafés, souvenir shops, museums, and tourists. But tilt your eyes up to the second and third floors, and you'll find ordinary people looking out on the street life and underwear drying on clotheslines. Although Cubans acknowledge openly that the system has its problems and corruptions, many people who vacate their buildings are able to return to live in their renovated apartments. The Office of the City Historian also made the renovation of the Old City a chance to provide employment for thousands of young people in the practice of restoration. Many of those students in the preservation trade schools live in Old Havana, so they are repairing buildings in their own neighborhoods, perhaps fixing their own homes to live in again.

The examples from Berlin and Havana suggest ways to create

Havana, Cuba, 2011
The Office of the City Historian owns all the buildings in Old Havana and has undertaken a massive preservation effort, luring tourists while retaining residents and training young people in building trades.

preservation programs that support equitable development. On a national scale, Americans should be launching a preservation wing of what economists such as Paul Krugman have proposed: a twenty-first-century version of the New Deal's Works Progress Administration. But this new WPA, the scholar Amber Wiley suggests, should have a different focus: "modernizing and maintaining existing buildings and infrastructure."[18] Much of the infrastructure needed for long-term economic health—roads, bridges, railways, tunnels, sewers, schools, parks, and housing— exists, but a good portion of it was built in the 1930s. Restoring the WPA legacy requires an investment of money and human labor. As anyone who crosses a bridge, goes to a state park, or drops off a child at school knows, the legacy of the 1930s WPA is still strong. Americans need to give those remarkable public investments another century.

On a local level, the model of IBA could be the vehicle for achieving this dream. IBA was Berlin's gift to itself in anticipation of the city's 750th anniversary in 1987. Imagine if New York had bestowed an "IBA" on itself as the response to the terrorist attacks of September 11, 2001. Instead of spending $2 billion on a spectacular memorial and museum beneath a 1,776-foot corporate headquarters to honor those who perished, city planners might have erected a dozen new schools and thousands of affordable apartments spread across the five boroughs, created by rehabilitating existing buildings and using the skills and labor of young people, to honor of the dead. Homage to the victims of the attacks would be paid when visitors hopped on buses that would take them around the city, whose vitality, enhanced by these new projects, would be the greatest memorial of all.

In arguing that preservation spending has a greater multiplier effect than other investments, suggesting that tax credits more than pay for themselves, and making the point that tourism dollars are often based on the existence of historic buildings, American preservationists have managed to make the movement a part of the growth coalition that characterizes urban development debates today. There is a trust—or at least a hope—that the free market can, with adequate incentives here and regulations there, be made to preserve America's heritage and promote healthy egalitarian development. While preservation does indeed "pay," there remains the question of whom it pays. In the process of fighting to be admitted to the club, where profit is the bouncer at the door, American preservationists have stepped back from some of the most powerful arguments for preservation in the struggle for economic justice. They must reclaim the part of their legacy that stands against the market as the measure of all things, and stand firmly again for the stewardship of place. From that position will flow a new ethos of preservation as a means by which to achieve a more equitable society.

5 preservation and sustainability

I live in a region that has more solar panels on its houses, more organic gardens, more community-supported agriculture farms, more tightly knit, pedestrian-based co-housing communities than almost anywhere in the United States. And we have a free public bus system. What we call the "Happy Valley" of western Massachusetts might even be able to compete with some cities in Europe in our carbon footprint.

But the greenest place in my valley is not my hometown, Amherst, or Northampton, another liberal paradise, but the city of Holyoke. A city with a glorious legacy but a deeply troubled present, Holyoke was one of America's first planned industrial communities, once the paper capital of the nation, home of National Paper and a dozen other paper companies, and at its height a city of 130,000 Irish, French Canadian, and Polish immigrants, who have more recently been joined by Puerto Rican and other Caribbean and Latin American immigrants and even Somalian refugees.

As companies fled to the union-free South, and then across the oceans, the tax base of Holyoke collapsed, and it has never recovered. Holyoke is one of the poorest cities in the Commonwealth of Massachusetts. Its school system is in receivership, it has an asthma rate three times the state average, and it faces problems of high crime, drug addiction, and hunger. Environmental Protection Agency "brownfield" sites dot the area because of the toxic soil and leftover machinery in its hulking factory buildings. One of the city's most glorious buildings, the railway station by the renowned architect H. H. Richardson, designer of Trinity Church in Boston, was a used-car-parts storage facility for thirty years. Nearby, rickety triple-decker houses overlook empty lots and boarded-up buildings. Brownfields, faded red brick, lots filled with rusted machinery—*green* is the last word that a casual observer would apply to Holyoke.

Holyoke earned its designation when the city was built, thanks to a decision to harness a powerful natural feature for its energy. The city bulges into the Connecticut River at South Hadley Falls. In the space of half a mile, the mighty Connecticut drops fifty-eight feet. By diverting the water from the dam upstream, then directing the flow gravitationally down through a series of canals, pushing the pressured water through narrow funnels underneath buildings, catching the rushing water with spinning

Factory and Canal in Holyoke, Massachusetts, 2013
The abandoned factories of Holyoke, once the papermaking capital of the country, are slowly being renovated. The water flowing through turbines underneath the buildings—visible on the right side of the photograph—produces clean energy that provides a majority of the city's electrical power.

paddles, and transforming that powerful spinning into electricity, Holyoke more than a hundred years ago created clean energy, which powered these mills in the nineteenth century, and now powers the electric lights and computers of the modern city. Together the dam and the system of canals produce 46 megawatts of energy, power 65 percent of the modern city's energy needs at some of the lowest rates in New England, and have a carbon footprint one-tenth the size of the average New England utility —all by harnessing the power of water going downhill using a system built over a century ago.[1]

In an era of climate change, when all around the world we are concerned about conserving energy and stopping the bellowing of pollutants into the air, when we are finally starting to rethink our reliance on fossil fuels and the automobile, we can find some answers in places like Holyoke.

The young, locally born mayor, Alex Morse, has brought attention to the city and pointed it in the right direction. Amtrak trains began stopping in Holyoke for the first time in decades. The canals are being spruced up to encourage development. In collaboration with the University of Massachusetts, the Massachusetts Institute of Technology, and CISCO Systems, the city built the Massachusetts Green High Performance Computing Center (MGHPCC)—essentially a computer farm, but the greenest computer farm in New England. Why did the consortium choose Holyoke? Because land was cheap there, but so was energy. Although the university and its partners missed a major restoration opportunity when they constructed a new building instead of renovating a historic one, they did build it in the downtown area, along the first level of canals, where it contributes to the return of activity to the city. Slowly private development is returning, although it mainly takes the form of small firms and artist studios that might foreshadow gentrification.

Holyoke is still in dire condition. Impoverished, with a pockmarked streetscape, as many buildings being torn down as going up, and little in the way of new jobs—a grand total of nine full-time people are needed for the operation of the MGHPCC—the city is in need of a more fundamental shift in attitude and policies if it is to recover. And this is where preservationists come in.

Preservationists can help rebuild the city by making the

case for preserving its industrial heritage, less on aesthetic grounds than in the interest of climate change: by saving Holyoke's sturdy nineteenth-century paper-industry buildings and taking advantage of the cheap clean energy produced by the 150-year-old canal system, the city will be building toward a more economically vibrant and environmentally sustainable future. Preservationists can tout Holyoke's history of sustainability, work for state and federal incentives to rebuild the buildings and infrastructure, and reorient its tax and development policies. People could begin to view Holyoke not through brown-tinted glasses but green ones. If preservationists make the case that the old housing and industrial stock could easily and affordably be adapted to present industrial and commercial needs, that the infrastructure and density of the buildings are valuable for the environment and the building of vibrant communities, then perhaps the city, with the necessary support from all levels of government, could make the shifts that would move development quickly and rapidly—like the waters rushing underneath the factories—toward the rehabilitation of America's greenest city.[2]

"We cannot build our way to sustainability; we must conserve our way to it." In 2007, the architect and sustainability activist Carl Elefante wrote these words in what has become one of the most cited articles on historic preservation. Richard Moe, former president of the National Trust for Historic Preservation, in the same vein argued, "Preserving a building is the ultimate act of recycling." And more recently, Daniel Bluestone, head of the preservation program at Boston University, has affirmed: "Historic preservation and adaptive reuse, not green building, should properly be conceived of as the keystone of sustainability."[3]

Since nearly half of all greenhouse gases are produced in the construction, demolition, and operation of buildings, saving old places and reusing them must be the cornerstone of any plan for sustainability. In other words, preservation of existing buildings is not simply a gesture but the centerpiece of the world's efforts to slow and ultimately reverse climate change. We will not make a dent in the crisis unless we focus more efforts on historic preservation. Preservation cannot be a hobby or an aesthetic movement. It has to be a key factor in the effort to save the planet. What have been seen as two separate movements—preservation and environmental conservation—will increasingly be seen as one and the same.

The 1966 National Historic Preservation Act was brought into the world by the same midwife that birthed the modern American environmental movement—anger at the despoliation of the physical and natural environment, reliance on government regulation but skepticism about government planning, and a healthy dose of grassroots empowerment. And yet, although the first section of the NHPA refers to the "energy benefits" of saving America's "irreplaceable heritage," the U.S. historic preservation movement took decades to embrace preservation's role in saving energy and fighting climate change.[4] The word *sustainability* was seldom heard in 1966, and no one realized that cars were changing the temperature of the earth. The preservation movement had as its clear purpose to save from destruction the nation's common archaeological, historical, and architectural heritage.

But it did not take long for the environmental movement to percolate into the preservation movement. Preservationists began making the case first for the value of preservation in energy conservation and later for slowing climate change as early as the 1970s. In 1980 a National Trust advertisement in national magazines pictured a three-story tenement building in the shape of a gasoline container. "It takes energy to construct a new building," reads the caption. "It saves energy to preserve an old one." Scholars and practitioners began to build a case for sustainability, focused on a network of related goals: the value of individual buildings for energy conservation; the relative cost-effectiveness of repairing older buildings; the importance of preserving older, denser, walkable neighborhoods and communities; and the need for people everywhere to reorient their approach to the human environment to be protective and supportive, rather than extractive.

Buildings arise through an enormous expenditure of energy. The longer the life of the building—the more use we get from the initial expenditure on building materials and construction—the less environmental impact the building will have. The initial burst of energy—mining the iron ore and turning it into steel, hacking down trees and turning them into timber frames, clearing the land for construction—becomes amortized over decades and even centuries until it virtually disappears. About half of all the energy needed for a building is expended in the initial extraction and transportation of materials, the erection of the structure, and the disposal of the waste; 20 percent is expended in mechanical and electrical systems; and 30 percent in a series of energy-expending activities, such as transportation of materials and manufacturing of furniture.[5] The National Trust's 2012 report offered an estimate of how long it would take a new building to "pay off" the climate impact of its initial construction. The range is wide, but it can take up to eighty years for a new, energy-efficient building to pay off its carbon debt. In other words, if the choice is to build a new, highly energy-efficient building or restore a strong-boned nineteenth-century building, the environmental answer is unambiguous: the new building might seem like a sustainable solution, but it actually contributes more to climate change than the old one. As the Preservation Green Lab argues, "The renovation and reuse of existing buildings of comparable functionality and size, and equivalent energy efficiency levels, consistently yield fewer environmental impacts than demolition and new construction over a 75-year period."[6]

Preserved older buildings contribute to the climate change solution by storing energy, serving, in essence, as carbon piggy banks. In contrast, the majority of "green" buildings being built today will not survive the years it will take to pay off their carbon debts: the amount they cost in carbon for their construction. Most buildings now are built for fifty-year lifespans and most do not even make it to that age, regardless of the structural materials used.[7]

Just as traditional preservation, focused on architectural and historical value, moved outward from the individual "gem" to "cultural landscapes," so too those making the case for preservation's centrality in energy conservation and climate change have moved beyond the individual building. Beginning with the work of Richard Moe and Carter Wilkie, whose *Changing Places: Rebuilding Community in the Age of Sprawl* (1997) was a watershed, calling for better-built communities in the face of widespread sprawl, preservationists increasingly argue for the preservation of dense older neighborhoods that emphasize walking and public transportation.[8]

Changing Places, like other reports that seek to place preservation at the center of climate change debates, took inspiration from the work of Jane Jacobs, who argued that vibrant, dense cities required older buildings. Jacobs has been seen as the godmother of the modern American preservation movement, helping to usher in the Landmarks Preservation Commission in New York and laying the groundwork for the movement's broader arguments for vital, dense cities. She fought successfully to preserve her Greenwich Village neighborhood from demolition and stood side by side with the architect Philip Johnson to protest the razing of Pennsylvania Station in 1963.

But Jacobs is an odd hero for preservationists. Her manifesto, *The Death and Life of Great American Cities,* contains little about preservation as it has come to be done in the United States for much of the past half century. Jacobs was not interested in the embodied energy of buildings, or in their historical or aesthetic values. Indeed, she had little concern—at least in terms of building and maintaining a healthy city—for "museum-piece old buildings." Rather, what she wanted were a "good lot of plain, ordinary, low-value old buildings, including some run-down old buildings."[9] Jacobs paid almost no attention to "historic" buildings in her argument about how to build economically vital cities. It was *old* buildings that mattered to her. "Cities need old buildings so badly," she wrote, "it is probably impossible for vigorous streets and districts to grow without them."[10] She saw old buildings as helping to maintain the streetscape of mixed building uses and, most important, as providing lower rents than newer buildings so that neighborhoods could maintain a mix of incomes and uses. A vibrant neighborhood needed wealthier residents in the new buildings, but it also needed space for an artist or a dockworker in the older buildings. Cities need old buildings, period.

Jacobs's later books, such as *The Economy of Cities* and *Cities and the Wealth of Nations,* may be far more relevant today than even her more famous first book. In these books Jacobs moves away from the micro-economy of the neighborhood, and her beloved Hudson Street, to examine the workings of an entire city's economy and then how cities function within a nation's economy. Jacobs was brilliantly prescient. Her argument about the centrality of cities to the national and world economy was only beginning to be proven accurate in the late 1960s when she wrote the second volume of her trilogy on cities. But today we live in an economy organized around a network of "world cities." Even as the preservation movement has grown in the United States over the past fifty years, the most important geographical phenomenon worldwide has been the growth of megacities. The world is, for the first time in its history, more urban than rural.

While many detractors, such as the left-wing urbanist Mike Davis, have highlighted the role of capitalism in creating a "planet of slums," others have suggested a powerful upside—people worldwide are living far more densely, and therefore more sustainably, because they are in cities. The *New Yorker* writer David Owen, in his *Green Metropolis,* taking New York, and especially Manhattan, as his model, argued that inhabitants of cities are more "green" than people elsewhere, no matter how well non-urbanites order their lives to be energy efficient and sustainable. Simply by living in smaller homes (i.e., apartments), in buildings tightly packed together (which prevents loss of heat), driving cars less often than people outside cities, and relying instead on walking and public transportation, inhabitants of cities use less energy than people who live in suburbs.[11]

Jacobs taught that a city cannot function well if it relies on voluntary acts of generosity, the kindness of strangers. She argued against "cataclysmic" urban renewal projects like the Lower Manhattan Expressway. Instead she encouraged small interventions that would make it "relatively simple," in her words, for ordinary people to participate in the safety and economic health of their city.[12] Preserving older buildings sets an economic engine in motion: stores and workplaces locate nearby; this encourages people to walk and fills the sidewalks, which makes the neighborhood safer; safe neighborhoods attract other businesses. Although she was an organizer and led the fight against urban renewal, at heart she was a believer in gently cajoling systems, applying oil to gears, and letting the capitalist machine run by itself. "Dull, inert cities," she wrote, "do contain the seeds of their own destruction and little else. But lively, diverse, intense cities contain the seeds of their own regeneration, with energy enough to carry over for problems and needs outside themselves."[13]

Advocates for preservation as a climate change strategy would agree. Since it appears to be inarguable that much higher densities are needed—both for energy conservation and to create more homes for burgeoning urban populations—the next questions might be, Should historic buildings of two, three, and even ten stories be swept aside in order to build towers of twenty, thirty, and forty stories? Will future cities look like those early-twentieth-century representations of New York: huge towers with a few historical "gems" set back in a park? The argument some have made is that with a growing world, we cannot preserve the density of a Greenwich Village—modest, even quaint, compared to many world cities—we need to rebuild our cities so that they have the density of Mumbai, Hong Kong, Lagos, or Tokyo. As it turns out, the answer to these questions is no. Tearing down and building anew presents more dangers to true sustainability—largely because of the crushing unlivability of some of these places—than the taller buildings and greater density would alleviate.

But at the same time that the National Trust and National Park Service and various researchers were making the case for preservation as a tool of sustainable living, mainstream American preservation practices continued to focus on the ideas embedded in the NHPA: which buildings to list, which to protect, how to rehabilitate them appropriately. I used to argue with Dorothy Miner, the irascible and incomparable lawyer for the Landmarks Preservation Commission in New York City, about preservationists' emphasis on "saving the gem." She said that just trying to put out the fires, to stop the rape and pillage by developers, was more than enough for ten lawyers like her working all day, every

Mong Kok, Hong Kong, 2013
Reputed to be one of the densest districts in the world—350,000 people
per square mile—Mong Kok, because its residents live so close
together, has a small carbon footprint.

day. Some of the other goals—such as interpretation of historic
places, such as climate change—would have to wait.

While the movement might deserve some criticism for its slow-
ness to join the fight against climate change, a greater measure
of blame for the situation in the United States is due to the relentless focus, in the construction world and at schools of architecture, on new buildings. The most popular—near ubiquitous
now—approach to "greening" a building or a campus or a town
in America is to build or adapt structures to comply with the
United States Green Building Council's LEED rating system.
The LEED (Leadership in Energy and Environmental Design)
system awards points for different actions that contribute to a

better environment. Architects and developers pull from a menu of options—a "green" roof consisting of soil and plants, recycled materials, solar panels—to get as close to one hundred points as possible. To earn a LEED "silver" rating a building needs to amass fifty points, "gold," sixty, and "platinum," eighty. The building gains seven points in the scale for providing access to public transportation. Two points for reducing outdoor water use. Two points for community outreach and involvement. Two points for a bicycle rack. Two points for historic resource preservation and adaptive reuse.[14] (Yes, putting up a bicycle rack to encourage riding to work is considered as valuable as not demolishing a historic building!)[15] There are other items of the LEED credit menu that encourage historic preservation. Credits are given, for example, for mixed-use neighborhoods and "smart locations," close to public transportation and other services, all of which lean in the direction of preserving historic buildings and neighborhoods. Historic buildings can even receive a "platinum" designation. With the advocacy of the Sustainable Preservation Coalition, LEED has changed its credit system. But even the latest edition fails to give preservation its rightful place near the top of the "green building" pyramid. The LEED rating system encourages high-tech solutions—"Gizmo Green," as one critic called it—giving a stamp of approval to projects that are in reality minimally green, and which undervalue both the embodied energy of historic buildings and their cultural value.[16] "LEED Platinum" is not the new green.

Perhaps the best contribution made by the LEED system is to have spurred the creation of better systems. Rather than lessen the

College of Environmental Science and Forestry,
State University of New York, Syracuse, 2013
The Gateway Center for SUNY-ESF is a LEED Platinum building.
But it will take decades of energy savings to equal the carbon expended
in the demolition of what it replaced and the construction of the new,
energy-efficient building.

carbon footprint of a building, there is a new push to build "net zero" buildings, structures that produce as much energy through passive and active technologies as they use. But even advocates of these solutions fail to give appropriate credit and encouragement to adaptive reuse. The Living Building Challenge (LBC), for example, appears to demand a higher level of sustainability in green building. Calling its program "the built environment's most rigorous performance standard," the LBC argues that net zero is not enough: "Nature doesn't do zero—it is net positive in energy, food, and flows."[17] Because of the rigor of the evaluation system, in 2015 there were only five certified LBC projects in the United States—one of those, the Bechtel Environmental Classroom, was built by Smith College; another is being built by Hampshire College in Amherst. Each of these is a new building that gained certification as a "living building" through a variety of means—but not through reusing older buildings. A similar movement in Germany, PassivHaus, deserves much praise for having developed a model that allows owners to dispense with high-energy conventional heating systems. By taking advantage of passive solar energy and developing tight building envelopes, practitioners have reduced the use of conventional heating and cooling systems to almost nothing. But this movement, too, does not encourage the reuse of old buildings.

All these efforts are moving us, slowly, in the right direction of living less toxically on our planet. But they all still start with the idea that we have to use technology to improve on the wasteful past. Windows are a perfect example. One of the first things that developers do, even in huge suburban homes that waste enormous amounts of energy, is install "high-efficiency" windows. These new windows, however, fail the environmental test, especially when compared to reused older windows, for a couple of reasons. It takes years before they will "pay back" the energy cost of their manufacture—not to mention that they are expensive to repair if they are broken. Furthermore, much of the energy loss through windows comes not through the glass but through the spaces around the windows, where the windows fit into the wall. Studies have shown that traditional windows, often built very tightly into walls, do a better job than new windows of preserving energy, and at a fraction of the cost.[18] Small changes—such as sealing roofs and basements and other obvious energy drains, easily found through an energy audit—would make the average house and commercial building even more energy efficient. As Richard Moe has written, "If 3,000 homes could be retrofitted each year, we estimate that after 10 years we could see a reduction of 65 million metric tons of carbon emitted into the atmosphere, and the equivalent of 200 million barrels of oil saved."[19]

In the United States, a deeper cultural problem lurks behind debates over windows and other retrofits. Most new attempts at green building take as a premise that new buildings must meet the current comfort levels that Americans demand and regulations require—maintaining a very narrow temperature range at all times of the year, somewhere between 68 and 76 degrees. Doing so requires the nearly constant operation of air conditioning and heating systems, which are more difficult to install and manage in historic buildings. This attitude—and the regulations—will have to change if Americans are truly to address climate change.

Many older buildings were designed with the climate in mind and do a remarkably good job in limiting energy use without advanced technology.

Hanging heavy curtains. Repairing old windows. Rejecting the fascination with new technology in favor of reuse. None of these strategies is taught in schools of architecture. Even schools with elite faculty who are knowledgeable about such matters do not require it of their design students. Most U.S. architecture schools arose during the modernist movement and retain the bias toward the new and contemporary. Preservation is seen as part of "community development" and is treated as a good way to show public spirit and interest in community engagement. But no one zooms to the top of the class at Harvard's Graduate School of Design or at Princeton's School of Architecture or at MIT by doing preservation. Indeed, almost none of the top American schools of architecture has a program in historic preservation. And programs in sustainability—all the rage in the first decades of the twenty-first century—rarely if ever place preservation at the core of their work. As Daniel Bluestone has written, the architectural profession was built on a modernist view that was antithetical to historic preservation. "Today," writes Bluestone, "50 years after Gropius' pronouncements and despite the rise of new urbanism, Postmodernism, and an ethic of sustainability, preservation architecture is still often treated with condescension and hostility."[20]

American design schools need to change their names to "schools of architecture and adaptive reuse." Until architecture schools demand that students study the principles and practices of historic preservation, and until they shift their orientation so most classes are focused around adaptation, reuse, and additions to historic structures, their dedication to "sustainability" will be empty rhetoric.

Not only architecture schools will have to change. Preservationists, too, if they really mean to lead the sustainability movement, will have to change. The U.S. preservation movement has recently begun making up for lost time, but it deserves some of the blame for being slow to understand the significance of conservation and environmentalism. Preservationists may not realize the implications to their monumental responsibility. To put it bluntly: if preservationists succeed in their quest to make preservation central to the climate change debate, the new movement will bear little resemblance to the current one. Why?

The reason is ironic: preservationists will finally have to be guilty of the charge they have long been accused of, but of which they were previously innocent. In the annals of attacks on advocates of preservation, the most common is "You want to save everything old." That accusation has not been true. But in the age of climate change, when preservationists have elbowed their way to the center of the conversation, it should now become true: preservationists should not be arguing solely for the preservation of beautiful or significant buildings; they must demand that Americans preserve most buildings. Tom Mayes of the National Trust has argued that America needs municipal bylaws that turn development rules on their head. In most places, the assumption is that developers or building owners can demolish their own property at will. Sometimes the only power local preservationists have—if they even have that—is a "demolition delay," a chance to keep the developer from demolition for thirty days or sometimes as long as a year. The hope is that during that time the developer will reconsider the project and preservationists will suggest a better alternative to demolition. Mayes suggests instead that cities and towns start with the assumption that all buildings should be renovated for new uses and demand that developers make a convincing case for the need to demolish them. The public interest in maintaining the embodied energy of a building—along with, in many situations, other values such as history and beauty—would supersede the owner's or developer's right to demolish it.[21]

Imagine this bylaw and the way of thinking it represents taking hold within the preservation world, down to local historical commissions. The orientation of the movement would shift from looking for exemplars of styles or particular sites of historic importance to seeing in each building from the past a possible key to a sustainable future and habitable planet. This would bring the U.S. preservation movement in line with the thinking of analysts like Michael Braungart and William McDonough, whose manifesto *Cradle to Cradle: Remaking the Way We Make Things* offers ideas that have still barely begun to influence the architectural world and the construction industry.[22] The "zero net energy" movement, Living Building Challenge, and PassivHaus have as a common belief that simply lowering the energy use of a building by 10, 20, or even 50 percent is not enough. Americans (indeed, everyone) should be building, and conserving, so that all their products yield no waste, but rather continue a cycle of use and resilience.

This way of thinking would also force American preservationists to work to upend one of the most popular forms of urban development of the past two decades—the massive demolition of thousands upon thousands of homes in cities such as Detroit, Baltimore, Philadelphia, and Cleveland to make way for new development. In Brooklyn Heights or South Philadelphia or the South End of Boston buildings are being lovingly restored and sold for millions. But often buildings of similar quality are being torn down as part of a pro-development strategy in other cities. The blocks of old buildings about which Jacobs waxes eloquent in *The Death and Life of Great American Cities,* which have inspired gentrification in other American cities from the 1980s to the present, are considered blighted territory when they stand in poor and minority areas. Baltimore's ubiquitous row houses are legendary for their elegant simplicity. But they were torn down by the hundreds throughout the 1990s as part of a city redevelopment effort; the city recently announced a plan to demolish four thousand more.[23] Jacobs anticipated the spread of this ideology in the example of Detroit, already in full free fall by 1960: "Detroit is largely composed, today, of seemingly endless square miles of low-density failure."[24]

These mass demolition efforts have long been criticized by planners as shortsighted, by preservationists as crimes against America's architectural history, and by community activists as a wasteful use of tax money. (Of course, there are also community activists who argue specifically in favor of demolition because of the dangers posed by dilapidated buildings, and their use as centers of illicit activity.) Now we can add to the case against wholesale demolition an environmentalist complaint: these policies are acts of environmental violence because of their unnecessary displacement of carbon into the atmosphere.

Preservationists must embrace and become advocates for each building becoming a generator of clean energy, not just an embodier of stored energy. Preservationists are often viewed as wind- and solar-energy skeptics, seeing wind turbines and solar panels as intrusions into a work of architecture or a historic landscape. If these could be hidden or minimalized, preservationists are likely to grudgingly go along with them. At Hancock Shaker Village in Pittsfield, Massachusetts, some preservationists were up in arms when the museum built a small solar array next to the entrance, so that before visitors came to a view of the famous round barn they would first pass this anachronism, with cows mingling around it. The Shakers are inaccurately regarded as having rejected new technologies. In fact, the solar array was in line with Shaker values, reflected not only in their elegant furniture but also in their sustainable practices of agriculture. The solar array was a modern continuation of the Shaker approach.

Closer to home, my university, the University of Massachusetts, Amherst, will soon install a huge solar array on the 650-foot-long, slanted, south-facing roof of the Fine Arts Center, one of the great buildings designed by the architects Kevin Roche and John Dinkeloo. There will no doubt be outcries that this solar array "destroys" the "integrity" of the architects' design. I disagree. Long ago, we came to accept fire escapes as necessary and required that they be added to old buildings. Handicap railings and ramps have followed more recently, because of a shift in law—the Americans with Disabilities Act of 1990—and in the culture. Because they were demanded by law, no one questioned the fact that a new ramp and railings would need to be added to the exterior of the nineteenth-century Old Chapel, the symbolic heart of the university. The addition did not even provoke words of regret—at least not publicly—because it was simply a required part of the renovation. Americans must equally accept and even celebrate the sight of solar panels and green roofs on every building—because the world is in a state of emergency. Historic buildings hold on to past energy, and their reuse prevents the expenditure of energy for new buildings.

American preservationists should be arguing for citywide and even nationwide statutes like those pioneered in Marburg, Germany, requiring all buildings, new and old, to have solar panels. While there were many who howled that this intrusion into private property portended a "green dictatorship," Germany can now boast that over half of its energy is generated by renewables. Lancaster, California, was the first U.S. city to require that new buildings have solar panels (as well as other energy- and environment-saving elements). But there should be far more. If we understand that there is a crisis—not just local or national, but global—we will all have to leave behind our resistance to solar panels, as the residue of a different age.[25]

Missing from any of the green rating systems that have proliferated in the United States and elsewhere in recent years is the calculus of love. Buildings that are cherished are more likely to be preserved, and we need to preserve not only buildings from the past but from the future past: the buildings we are constructing now and need to have around, embodying their energy, a hundred years from now. The architect Stephen Mouzon has written that "buildings cannot be sustainable if they are not lovable."[26] Buildings, no matter how technologically advanced, that are not loved will easily be disposed of once the technological fad of the moment has passed, or its energy-efficiency achievements are superseded by the next decade's inventions. There is no simple way to know what buildings will garner affection, and protection, a century or two from now. But when we build new structures and expect them to be demolished and replaced within fifty years—the standard among many U.S. companies and institutions—then we are not even giving them a chance to pay back their carbon debt to society and begin contributing to a more sustainable planet. And odds are good that buildings designed for a short lifespan will not be designed to be loved over the long term.

The U.S. preservation movement must lead the fight to make preservation central to architecture programs, to make preservation more valued in LEED and other energy-efficiency systems, to loosen its own Secretary's Standards, which contribute to the view that preservation and rehabilitation pose obstacles to sustainability instead of opportunities for it. Preservationists should be at state hearings calling for more rail transportation. They must argue for systems that minimize carbon emissions. They should promote tax incentives and zoning changes that give a strong, legal push back toward traditional city centers, not simply to bring jobs to those places, but because those places are greener than other places. They need to support bringing greater density to suburbs and exurbs, as well as to the city centers of large cities. These kinds of actions will promote the return to cities and the valuing of historic places.

Building a sustainable—a survivable—world requires many changes in our attitudes, and saving historic buildings is just one of them. We need to change our fundamental goal so that in every action we are thinking about how we are affecting the local and global environment. At the heart of this is strengthening the frayed bonds of emotional and social connection between individuals and the places they inhabit. We do this in part by returning democracy to the preservation equation, by building a movement that celebrates "places that matter," in the words of Place Matters, an innovative organization in New York City, and seeks to document, celebrate, and tell the history of those places through conversations among citizens. Nature and culture converge in the specifics of place, and the places that matter most to communities are often the ones they hold in common. When Americans talk about building "sustainable communities," they are looking at something much broader than preventing flooding or generating renewable energy. They want to learn how to nurture and support their total environment, to create healthy communities in the broadest sense.[27] This is preservation's ultimate contribution to the sustainability crisis: it provocatively asks, What are the places that matter to us? What are the stories people have told about these places, and the stories they will tell in the future? The answers are what give all of us a sense of rootedness in time and place, and make us value those places as we value our homes and our families.

For most of us, it is not possible to re-create the connections we once had. We cannot inhabit Martin Heidegger's beloved Black Forest homestead, about which he wrote soon after World War II, which was built within a cohesive religious culture that sheltered the mundane and sacred together. His world no longer exists. But the quest for belonging, tied in part to landscape and architecture, to history, and to familiarity, certainly persists. Indeed it has gained strength because the landscape we have created does not allow memory to find a purchase. "The trick," writes the long-time *New Yorker* essayist Tony Hiss, "is to get our many conservation and preservation groups, each a bright, shining star, to see themselves as forming a single constellation of protection. They can start by acknowledging that at the deepest level they both unlock the same door. Both a train station and a tree, that is, can shake us out of the daydream that the present moment is disconnected from all the lives that preceded us and all the life around us."[28]

6

preserving and interpreting difficult places

Among the carefully selected volumes I brought with me to Rome when I lived at the American Academy was a book that seemed relevant neither to the city nor to my topic of preservation—Naomi Klein's *Shock Doctrine: The Rise of Disaster Capitalism.* But toward the close of the book, Klein reflects on the role of memory in returning power to the people of Latin America and other places where the "shock troops" of free-market, privatization ideologies have left disaster in their wake. One tool of the shock doctrine has been the "erasure—of history, of culture, of memory": "All shock therapists are intent on the erasure of memory," she writes. "Memory, both individual and collective, turns out to be the greatest shock absorber of all."[1]

In the public eye, historic preservation is concerned with the beautiful, the heroic, and the uplifting. Historic preservation, the everyday work of local historical commissions in America and other nations, has been centrally about saving beautiful buildings, marking the homes of heroes, curating sites of valor, helping to anchor citizens in time and place them in a continuum of family and nation. Historic sites matter because they raise us up—spiritually, culturally, personally. These reasons for saving our old places are all true and right, and preservationists' work benefits all humanity.

But Klein introduces another value: the importance of preserving and interpreting "difficult places," the places of pain, of violence, of controversy, the places we normally want to avoid. Part of the calling of preservation is to help societies confront their difficult places and difficult pasts, to contribute to the fundamental human needs for memory and justice.

Over the past several decades, the world has experienced a quiet revolution. Places where violence and discrimination occurred, where resistance to those evils took hold, have been marked, listed, interpreted. Existing historic sites that long tried to erase the crimes of the past have been reimagined with layered stories. I think of childhood visits to Monticello or to Magnolia Plantation outside Charleston, where the word *slavery* was rarely uttered and a lone slave cabin stood in the parking lot with a sign that defended the homes of the slaves as being little different from the childhood home of Abraham Lincoln. Now Magnolia's slave cabins are being rebuilt and included as part of the standard tour at the site. The National Park Service has undertaken theme studies that touch on the violent battles between capital and labor, against Latin American and Japanese immigrants.

Nowhere has the change been so poignant for me as in Money, Mississippi, a town that seems little more than a train depot. In 1955 a black youth, Emmett Till, was beaten beyond recognition for the crime of allegedly whistling at the wife of the owner of a general store, and his murderers were all acquitted in a southern court. This event energized the American civil rights movement. When I first saw that store it was a ruin, its shell barely standing. But when I returned a few years later a marker stood out front, claiming it as part of Mississippi's Freedom Trail, with full-color images and a straightforward, accurate history of the boy's murder. Nothing was visible outside the courthouse in Sumner, where the travesty of justice was played out. The monument to the Confederate soldier still stood guard. Nonetheless, the state had decided—under pressure from new histories, a documentary, and the anniversary of the murder—to put its official imprimatur on this dusty site in the Delta. From the National Register and the National Trust to the local Tulsa Reparations Coalition, which is fighting to memorialize and repair the damage wrought by the 1921 Tulsa race riot, there is a nationwide demand for making what was hidden visible. Preservationists have recently come to embrace a belief in what Avishai Margalit calls "the healing power of knowing the truth."[2]

Preservation movements worldwide have begun to feel the distant ripples of the revolutions of the 1960s and to heed the demands for social justice in a wide range of arenas and the rising voices of an ever more diverse citizenry. The institutional embodiment of the maturity of the movement was the founding in 1999 of the International Coalition of Sites of Conscience. Starting with seventeen members, the coalition now includes more than two hundred sites of conscience around the world. Both the Manzanar internment camp in California and the Sacred Ground Historical Reclamation Project in Richmond, Virginia, are members, as are diverse places and institutions like New York City's Lower East Side Tenement Museum (one of the founding organizations); the National Women's Rights Memorial in Seneca Falls, New York; the Iroquois Indian Museum in Howes Cave, New York; Hawaii's King Kamehameha V Judiciary History Center in Honolulu; Lowell National Historical Park in Massachusetts; and Eastern State Penitentiary in Philadelphia. Around the world, members range from human rights organizations to museums, including the Casa de la Memoria in Colombia, the Apartheid Museum in South Africa, the Gulag Museum in Russia, and the Liberation War Museum in Bangladesh.

The movement to create sites of conscience has not simply been a call to expand the list of buildings we call "historic." As Ned Kaufman has argued, we cannot just identify new "difficult places"; we need to reinterpret existing historic sites to reveal their place within the web of relationships of power that created them.[3] At the 2015 gathering of preservationists at Kykuit, the Rockefeller estate owned and run by the National Trust, I took the standard tour of the building, led by Historic Hudson Valley. I learned a lot about the architecture and landscape, as well as about John D. Rockefeller's art collection and his generosity in sending small sums to individuals who wrote to him for financial assistance. But I learned nothing about how Rockefeller acquired his money, his relationship with labor unions, and other, more controversial matters. Avoiding these subjects is not just a missed opportunity, but a continuing shame, a daily whitewashing of history, no matter how pleasantly done.

There is a second, crucial, aspect to the movement to develop and interpret sites of conscience. (Preservationists and allied organizations have adopted a more generic term for these—"difficult places"—but something may have been lost in translation.) Liz Ševčenko, one of the founders of the International Coalition (and now head of the Humanities Action Lab at the New School for Social Research), argues that at the heart of the movement is using places to foster conversations about the past, with an eye toward action in struggles of the present. "A site of conscience is not just where something bad happened," she insists. The difference is in how the stewards of the site—a grassroots group or a national museum—use the historic site to promote ongoing discussion. "Where the rubber hits the road," says Ševčenko, is in fostering dialogue on an ongoing basis and making that central to the work of the museum, site, or organization.[4]

A rapidly growing number of U.S. institutions, organizations, museums, and national parks have joined the movement to preserve and interpret the difficult histories of their sites. The challenge to them and other organizations is to go beyond the wish and make it a reality. Many countries have begun this kind of work with their own difficult places, and Americans have much to learn from the curators of these places, which have been the sites of violent and sustained upheavals in the past century. These interpreters have confronted that past, demonstrating the dangers of forgetting and pioneering moving and forceful ways of making memory matter for personal and national reconciliation, and as a step toward achieving justice. Two places in which they have been particularly successful are Berlin and Buenos Aires. But I'll start this brief journey around the world in Rome, which offers a cautionary tale.

From atop the Janiculum, where Giuseppe Garibaldi fought unsuccessfully for the independence of the city in 1849, visitors can look out at centuries of ambitious visions for the city. Squint a little and you can see the monuments of Roman emperors: the Baths of Diocletian, the Pantheon, the Palatine Hill. Later planners were popes, usually scions of wealthy Roman families, who erected the city that is so recognizable today, a city of palazzi and church domes, of grand squares and obelisks.

As virtually no modern buildings have been added to the city's historic center since the 1950s, a visitor might easily get the sense that Rome has remained largely unchanged for centuries. This is not the case. It has undergone many changes, and one of the most extensive rebuilders, Benito Mussolini, radically transformed the city in the twentieth century. Mussolini and his stable of architects and planners built post offices, sports facilities for youth, apartments and schools, public markets. They remade the road system, not only blasting out the massive via dei Fori Imperiali, but also the via della Conciliazione, the equally famous boulevard leading to Saint Peter's Square. They built entire new towns in agricultural lands south of Rome, made possible by the massive draining and reclaiming of the Pontine marshes.

Some of the most surreal sights in modern Rome are Mussolini's surviving spectacles of propaganda. To the south of the city is the site of the planned EUR—the Esposizione universale Roma, the 1942 world's fair—a necropolis of white neoclassical forms, including an abstract, cubelike homage to the Colosseum, all part of an unfinished celebration of twenty years of fascism. The Foro Mussolini (now the Foro Italico), a sports facility north of the Vatican, features a mosaic plaza—the largest built since the fall of Rome—celebrating the colonial conquest of Ethiopia in 1936. The mosaic includes 248 crumbling but still legible repetitions of the favorite roar at fascist rallies: "IL DUCE." Visitors in search of the balcony where Mussolini used to inflame the cheering crowds in piazza Venezia will find no notice directing them to it, no information about it. Everyone who visits the square looks up—never was there a leader who used balconies to greater effect—but access to it is blocked to the public.[5]

The buildings, the most visible aspect of Mussolini's legacy, have undergone a bit of intellectual laundering: a growing number of people argue that fascist-era architecture—especially that displaying a modernist, or "rationalist" aesthetic—should be judged on its own aesthetic terms. With the exception of the overtly propagandistic buildings, "brutalist" architecture should not be linked to the values of the regime that built them. Especially loved are the works of Luigi Moretti, who built sleek modernist buildings for the regime in Rome. His GIL building, a former sports center named for the Gioventù italiana del littorio

Mosaic in the Foro Italico, Rome, 2014

The sports stadium was one of Mussolini's grandest propaganda projects
of the 1930s. The 1960 Olympics were held there, and today, on their way
to soccer matches, thousands walk over the mosaic in which Mussolini's
nickname Il Duce, "the leader," is repeated 248 times.

(organization of Italian fascist youth) has been lovingly restored, down to the bronze eagles (Mussolini's faux-imperial standard) over the front entrance. Although Moretti was a devout follower of Mussolini, he was "rehabilitated" after the war and continued to receive commissions, including one for a dramatic apartment complex in the U.S. capital: the Watergate. Paolo Nicoloso, a leading historian of Mussolini's architecture, argues that the renewed, and sometimes nostalgic, appreciation of Mussolini's buildings of stone and marble is understandable in the context of Italy's long postwar economic decline: "When Italian people see a monumental building they are grateful to Mussolini. They believe he did well for the people. They forget the dictatorship, the racial laws, the war." Rome, and Italy more generally, engages in a form of organized forgetting.[6]

Such attitudes might matter only to debates about Rome's cultural heritage, were it not that fascism remains strong in Italy. Mussolini still has a constituency, and a growing one. The popularity of Italy's former prime minister Silvio Berlusconi is due in part to the way he invoked the personality and imagined accomplishments of Il Duce. Mussolini's granddaughter holds a Senate seat. Rome's mayor from 2008 to 2013, Giovanni Alemanno, was closely identified with the fascist movement. Swastikas, too, are common graffiti seen around Rome, targeting rival sports teams and politicians as well as Jewish leaders. Mussolini's own image rarely makes an appearance—his pictures were removed in a spasm of antifascism after the war—but throughout the city visitors can spot hundreds of copies of the ancient Roman military emblem that gave fascism its name. The fasces—a bundle of sticks with an ax—was affixed to public buildings, fountains, manhole covers, even doorstops during Mussolini's dictatorship. Many were removed after the war, but, as is typical here, the removal was inconsistent and dependent on the politics of neighborhoods. In Germany, the swastika has been outlawed, and it cannot be seen in public spaces. But in Italy, the fasces remain sprinkled throughout the urban landscape.

Mussolini came from the north and once disdained the Eternal City, but after he seized power in his 1922 coup he remade the urban landscape as only a few before him had done. Today he might be surprised, and pleased, to see how little of his legacy has been erased. It is not even discussed. Public reckonings are central to how other nations have moved forward from morally repugnant pasts. Not so in Italy. Today a handful of people are trying, openly, to confront Mussolini's architectural imprint on Rome, but they make up a small minority. "When I walk across the bridge to go to the soccer stadium and I see 'Mussolini Dux' on that obelisk, I want to blow it up," the famed historian of the resistance to fascism, Alessandro Portelli, told me. But a far more common response to the debate about Mussolini's legacy is the one described by Rosalia Vittorini, the head of the Italian chapter of DOCOMOMO, an organization that fights to preserve modern architecture around the world. In a café in the piazza Augosto Imperatore, I asked her what Romans think when they walk by a fascist building, or sit, as we were, in a building built expressly to proclaim his vision for a Third Roman Empire. She responded simply, "Why do you think they think anything at all?" [7]

Some Italians do think about it, and they are working to make the memory of that time part of the urban landscape, with a nervous intensity born of concern about the rise of right-wing movements across Europe. Siblings Adachiara and Luca Zevi, children of the Jewish modern architectural historian and critic Bruno Zevi, have separately taken on projects to remind Romans of the dark side of their recent history. Adachiara and her Arte in Memoria Foundation have brought the German activist Gunther Demnig to install some of his *stolpersteine*—bronze cobblestones set in front of the homes where Jews of the Nazi era once lived. In Italy, the stolpersteine are placed in front of the homes of Romans (largely but not exclusively Jews) who were persecuted and later, starting in October 1943, deported to Nazi death camps.

Luca has designed a Holocaust memorial museum that will be built in a park adjacent to Villa Torlonia, an eighteenth-century country estate located a mile beyond the walls of ancient Rome. Interpreters of the villa gloss over some of its historical incarnations, especially the period in which Mussolini lived there, during much of the 1920s and 1930s, often with his Jewish mistress. This silence is the more disturbing because the village sits atop Mussolini's personal bunker and a Roman-era Jewish catacomb system; nearby is the private English school that now educates Mussolini's great-grandson, son of his granddaughter Alessandra Mussolini, the senator. Finally, after years of arguing with the city bureaucracy, the South African artist William Kentridge was able to complete his project of drawing ninety huge figures of "victory and lament" from Roman history along the high walls that channel the Tiber River near the Vatican. One of those will be an image copied from a Naples mural that still stands, shot through with World War II bullet holes, of Mussolini on a horse, like the imperial Roman leaders he so admired, giving his infamous salute.

While these efforts inspire hope, they are few and fragile. When it comes to Mussolini's legacy, one of the world's great cities has largely looked the other way. Serious critical reflection on fascism in Rome is relegated to history books and outliers on the political left. There is no museum where visitors can learn about Italian fascism. This leaves Romans with a hazy understanding of the period, and that ignorance has provided an opening for disturbing revisionist sentiment about a leader who, in the last years of a twenty-year reign, tied his future and that of his people to Hitler. In a country faced with long-term economic weakness and an influx of immigrants from around the Mediterranean, the silent witness of fascist buildings offers mementos of Italy's former strength to the resurgent right. In an Italy and a Europe rumbling with the newfound power of the right wing, the more typical response to the fascist past is a deafening silence.

BERLIN: A THOUSAND YEARS OF NEVER FORGETTING

Silence is one word we cannot apply to Berlin.

For me as an individual, and, I believe, for the art of remembering the worst moments of our history, Berlin looms large. I have a long and troubled relationship with this city, with which my family has been engaged for nearly a century. My father's connection to Berlin began in 1926, when he moved with his family from Košice, Czechoslovakia, to what was then the economic and cultural capital of Europe. But he fled in 1937, well into the Nazi reign. Welcomed residents, hated outcasts, eager tourists, skeptical observers, academic collaborators, business partners—my family has played many roles in this city.

Berlin, the center of the Nazi regime and the apparatus of the Holocaust, conveniently pushed aside the memory of its recent past in the aftermath of World War II. But under pressure from a new generation and politically engaged artists, Berlin has taken on the task of building a memorial landscape as virtually no other city has done. Berlin's obsession with history and memory embodies one of the hallmarks of our age. It also defines a nation—at least a capital city—that is firmly committed to the mantra "Never forget." With each visit to Berlin, I see new memorials, new efforts to interpret sites related to Hitler and his regime. If the ubiquitous clutter of memorials annoys some visitors, it is a far better failing than silence.

German artists and memorial makers have for two generations been committed to not creating what they call *Kranzwerfstellen.* This German word, which translates as "wreath-throwing places," captures the failure of so many memorials, even those that consciously try to remain relevant. In the words of the Austrian writer Robert Musil, "There is nothing in this world as invisible as a monument": the man on the horse, the obelisk, the stone marker—all are attempts at permanence, but most quickly become forgotten.[8] Desperate to make memory last, and deeply suspicious of the history of jingoist monuments, German artists and architects of the postwar period went about the job of remembering the Holocaust and its Nazi makers by building counter-monuments—interventions at historic sites that could not be brushed aside, would not admit of one-line summaries, do not allow viewers to get away with dropping a simple tear and moving on. In Berlin, visitors stumble over the stolpersteine, visit the Jewish Museum of Daniel Libeskind, which embodies in its design the shattered history of Jews and Germans, and climb to the top of the transparent dome of the Reichstag to look down into the parliament hall Hitler burned, where now a democratic government works.[9] And perhaps they will come across the piercing silence of Micha Ullman's *Library* in Bebelplatz—a glass square etched out of a wide stone plaza in front of the prestigious Humboldt University on Unter den Linden. Within it lies a room of white empty bookshelves, marking the place where "degenerate" books were burned in the 1930s and memorializing the lost books and murdered people.

The work of memory continues. The unwillingness in many countries—Spain, Hungary, Ukraine, Japan—to acknowledge the truth of the atrocities of the past century makes the insistence in Berlin, and Germany generally, not to forget and not to gloss over the past all the more impressive. The monument to the Roma and Sinti peoples (and the subtle but significant changes to the language of the "documentation center" beneath the Holocaust memorial) is the latest effort to explore and acknowledge the Nazi extermination strategies in their entirety. This new memorial, which sits inside the Tiergarten between the Brandenburg Gate and the Reichstag, is officially part of the Foundation for the Memorial to the Murdered European Jews; it

Bebelplatz, Berlin, 2014

The Israeli artist Micha Ullman's *Library* memorial across from Humboldt University. In the Nazi era, "degenerate" books were burned in the square. Ullman's memorial is a ten-by-ten-foot room with empty white bookshelves, suggestive of the burned books, which foreshadowed cremated people.

is an adjunct of the Holocaust memorial, constructed after advocates, and politicians with consciences (or guilt feelings), eventually succeeded in forcing recognition for the 500,000 Roma and Sinti who were targeted and murdered.

In Berlin, to ignore the Nazi past, visitors and citizens would have to willfully look the other way.

BUENOS AIRES: MEMORY IN THE SERVICE OF JUSTICE

If Germany's memorial efforts have been in the service of not forgetting, in Buenos Aires, human rights activists use memory to achieve long-denied legal justice. Their memorials identify the sites of the 1970s state terror as crime scenes and the perpetrators as criminals yet to be punished.

Old military schools, neoclassical police stations, Gothic churches, French-inspired mansions, and rural estancias: these were the torture centers of Argentina's "Dirty War" of 1976–83. Operating within the elegance of the turn-of-the-twentieth-century "Paris of South America," the state terrorism (a better description of what happened there than "dirty war") of the 1970s was centrally organized but widely dispersed, based on a network of hundreds of detention and torture centers in neighborhoods across the city and nation. State terrorism was an everyday system of repression. The Argentine government was more paranoid about left-wing movements, and more committed and organized in its repressive policies, than the governments of Chile, Uruguay, Bolivia, and Brazil, the other nations linked together in Operation Condor—the U.S.-supported effort to violently suppress leftist movements in South America. [10]

Argentina has since the 1990s gone through a delayed national reckoning with the era of state terrorism. Human rights groups formed to combat the efforts of conservative regimes of the 1980s and 1990s to "put the past in the past." The regime of Carlos Menem, who served as president from 1989 to 1999, put an end to state prosecution of those involved in the torture and insisted on closure through erasure. Menem proposed that sites related to the dictatorship, such as the detention center at the School of the Navy Mechanics (ESMA), be razed as acts of "national reconciliation." But after Néstor Kirchner was elected

The School of the Navy Mechanics (ESMA), Buenos Aires, 2010
Some five thousand people were imprisoned, tortured, and ultimately taken
to their deaths from this military school in a well-to-do neighborhood of
Buenos Aires.

president in 2003 he reopened the debate about how that time and those crimes should be remembered. Kirchner (who was followed in the presidency by his wife, Cristina Fernández de Kirchner) was much more sympathetic to the victims and built political support on the left in part by demanding new accountability for the perpetrators and new respect for the victims and their families.

Argentina is "supremely enigmatic," wrote the historian Marguerite Feitlowitz in her magisterial *Lexicon of Terror*. A nation of enormous wealth, high literacy, and impressive scientific and industrial achievements, Argentina has had through much of the twentieth century a propensity toward "self-destructive" politics, she argued, in the form of violent coups.[11] But in its citizens' quest to remember, recall, warn, and demand, Argentina today is also at the forefront in wrestling with the issue of how to preserve sites of national disgrace, to remember the bad times and honor the victims. Just as the dictators warned in the 1970s, Argentina has been the vanguard of the left, if not in the ways the regimes of the 1970s predicted. Argentina's artists and human rights activists, family members of the *desaparecidos* (the "disappeared"), and graffiti muralists have forced their country to confront the era of state terrorism, and they have inspired a similar process in Chile, Uruguay, Guatemala, and Brazil. In doing so, they have drawn on an international trade in memorial ideas over the past three decades. The *baldosas,* colorful tiles which mark with great simplicity the homes of those who were disappeared, were inspired by Gunter Demnig's stolpersteine. The national memorial to the disappeared, with its wall of names, is impossible to imagine being conceived without Maya Lin's Vietnam Veterans Memorial in Washington, D.C. Argentina's citizens and artists have taken these ideas and made them their own.

Thirty-five years after the naval mechanics training school was founded in the elegant northern section of Buenos Aires, the main building, once the largest detention and torture site in the city, serves as a historic site and museum, while the rest of the school buildings have been turned over to various human rights groups. Just a mile to the east is the vast Parque de la Memoria (Memory Park), the national memorial to the disappeared. More than ten thousand names are inscribed on a winding wall; it was designed to allow names to be added as bodies were discovered across the

16 Tons, Caseros Prison, Buenos Aires, 2009
Artist Seth Wulsin knocked out selected glass brick windows in the notorious
and now demolished Caseros Prison, creating pixelated portraits of some of
the political prisoners. (Image courtesy of the artist.)

country, often in mass graves. In addition to official commemorations, popular, grassroots memorials and public art installations flourish on the sidewalks and walls across this sprawling city. And all the clandestine detention centers, as well as hundreds of individual memories, have now been documented in Memoria Abierta's guidebook to the city, *Memories in the City: Signs of State Terrorism in Buenos Aires.*[12]

This landscape of memory was the result in part of a judicial system that was hijacked: prosecutions of the culprits ended just two years after the end of the dictatorship, in 1985, as a way to move toward reconciliation; many of those convicted were later pardoned under the more conservative Menem regime. With one avenue closed, grassroots organizations found other ways to keep up the drumbeat for justice. The memorial interventions were not simply acts of memory, ways of looking back. They were political acts, means of keeping alive the fact that there would be no closure until the perpetrators, many of whom still resided in Buenos Aires's wealthy northern suburbs, had been punished in a court of law.

The activists' effort have borne fruit. At the end of 2009 some of the key leaders of the military dictatorship were finally forced to appear before a judge or were brought into court again after having been pardoned. In the spring of 2012, with the conviction of Jorge Videla, the dictator who led the coup in 1976, as well as of other leaders and military officials who conspired to steal some five hundred children from their imprisoned mothers, Argentinians finally saw evidence that closure might be imminent. The conviction of the most notorious perpetrators led one of the stolen children, Victoria Montenegro, who learned of her true identity thirty years after her kidnapping, to declare: "With this verdict we are repairing what happened." Because of the work of human rights activists, including preservationists, Argentina is confronting its past and bringing the perpetrators to justice.

The act of repair—or "making one whole," as legal briefs frequently call for—is often seen as the work of the courts. In the debates over public history and the pain of remembering the difficult pasts of nations and communities, we often separate public memory from procedural justice. Prosecutions and truth commissions must do the state's work of bringing the guilty to justice, while artists and community members must remember and recall, healing families and communities. Artists and activists create baldosas and national memorials as a way of recalling the past and coming to terms with it. The people of Buenos Aires are remembering their loved ones and also bearing witness to the evil perpetrated by their political leaders, sometimes with citizens' silent complicity. The work of preservation, public art, and memorialization is to peer into the past, both to provide solace and to warn future generations.

In Buenos Aires, the artistic efforts to expand public memory were part of an effort to create the conditions for procedural justice in the present. When that effort succeeded, Argentinians could finally look ahead to a world beyond these crimes and victims. The punishment of the guilty and the prospect of a new Argentina were made possible by the memorial efforts of grassroots activists over the course of three decades. They redeemed the rule of law and the honor of their nation.

THE UNITED STATES: CITIZEN SURGEONS AT WORK

The roar is constant, a pounding surf. Cars by the tens of thousands rush through downtown Richmond, Virginia, on I-95, bringing travelers north to Washington, D.C., to New York, to New England, or south to North Carolina, to Georgia, to Disney World. Passengers daydreaming about where they are going sel-

Shockoe Bottom, Richmond, Virginia, 2015

An image of Lumpkin's Jail, where slaves were held, bought, and sold in one of the largest slave markets in the United States, sits below Interstate 95, and in the shadow of the White House of the Confederacy, now enclosed by buildings of Virginia Commonwealth University Medical Center.

dom think about what they are passing through—and over. The site adjacent to the highway and the commercial core of the city was most recently a parking lot for the nearby Virginia Commonwealth University (VCU) Medical Center. But long before that, hidden underneath the grass and soil of two centuries, is a place almost everyone seems to have forgotten until recently: a burial ground for enslaved Africans who died in prison or awaiting sale. This is Shockoe Bottom, after New Orleans the largest marketplace for buying and selling African slaves in the United States. The memories of this place had almost disappeared until the Sacred Ground Historical Reclamation Project decided to reclaim both the site and its history. The leader of the group, Ana Edwards, states the organization's justification simply: "We have the right to know."[13]

The pressure of the wind is relentless as air is channeled between the Sierra Nevada and Inyu mountain ranges down through Owens Valley, California. Visitors feel it as they try to walk and are buffeted like tumbleweed. That's what the oral histories and the novelists describe as well, in memories shared about Manzanar, where more than ten thousand Japanese Americans were held, imprisoned, interned—the choice of verb carries its own weighty struggle—behind barbed wire beginning just months after Japan's attack on Pearl Harbor and through the end of World War II.[14] Amid dusty former roads, many overgrown with desert flowers, beside the now-absent lines of barracks, mess halls, and public latrines, alongside orchards of the prewar town, visitors will also find something else: Japanese gardens built by

Manzanar Japanese Internment Camp, Lone Pine, California, 2015
Ten thousand Japanese Americans were imprisoned here during World
War II. Most of the camp's buildings were torn down, leaving signs to
tell passersby what once stood here. In other places, dusty remnants of
Japanese gardens built by the inmates are slowly being uncovered by
park staff and descendants.

the men and women forced to make their homes here, and curving pools and stones resonant with religious symbolism.

The soft breeze delights and the sound of birds chirping starts, as if on cue, as visitors reach a hilltop off state highway 18 in southern Utah, an hour's drive north of the town of Saint George, the winter home of Brigham Young, the founder of the Church of Jesus Christ of Latter-day Saints (the Mormons). There is little to see at Mountain Meadows now: the blood and bones of 140 murdered men, women, and children, emigrants from Arkansas in an earlier September 11 massacre have been absorbed into unmarked graves across the valley at the spots where they were murdered. On that day in 1857, after a several days' standoff, the migrants were killed by a still-controversial and undetermined combination of Mormon militia and Paiute Indians, both of whom may have been directed by the church leadership under Young. Fearful of federal power, and unsettled by tensions over slavery and paranoia about immigrants of all types, church leaders seem to have encouraged a deep suspicion of eastern migrants passing through Mormon territory.[15] At the top of the hill, there is a stone memorial naming all the victims. Viewing stations allow visitors to survey a landscape of memorials, built by the Mormon church, which has chosen to acknowledge its role in the massacre, one of the worst of its kind.

These three very different historic sites—a paved-over, long-forgotten burial ground in the middle of a city; a national park complex in a desert valley; a landscape of memorials on a mountainside—represent three types of historical crime in the United States. A centuries-long history of violence and degradation against an enslaved people. A one-day massacre with religious overtones. A concentration camp—that's what President Franklin Roosevelt, who created it, called it—rooted in racism, where few died but all were marked for life.

All three "difficult places" also have much in common. Each place was intentionally covered over in order to hide the shame it bore witness to. Each historical marker is the product of grassroots action, starting with preservationists (who might not have called themselves preservationists), demanding action by institutions—the city of Richmond, the Latter-day Saints, the federal government—to save a place, mark a site, right a wrong. All three sites have come alive only in the past two decades. Until 1997, visitors would have found a lone memorial at Mountain Meadows, and no acknowledgment by the Mormons of the church's role in the massacre. And only in that that same year was land acquired by the federal government to create a National Historic Site at Manzanar; the full exhibition did not open until 2004. Until 2010, when small markers were installed, virtually nothing identified the site of Lumpkin's Jail in Shockoe Bottom, the lone physical remnant of the slave market complex. And even that was endangered by a proposed minor league baseball stadium project and other development.

But most of all, these three sites offer examples and exemplars of a new commitment to uncovering the places of pain and shame in the American landscape, one of the most important developments in the historic preservation movement in the past three decades. Focusing on the difficult places in the American story is giving preservation more relevance to a new generation, especially to groups most skeptical of its value. But although "difficult places" and "sites of conscience" may increasingly be heard among preservationists, this work has just begun.

The memorials spread across several miles at Mountain Meadows represent an important station on the road to bringing the truth of the atrocity out into the open. But for many—descendants and critics of the Latter-day Saints—the site represents a frustrating battle of incomplete recognition and reconciliation. The church long tried to deflect blame. But starting in 1999 and then more robustly in 2007, it has acknowledged responsibility for the massacre.

For unknowing visitors, the series of memorials set in the glorious landscape conveys a moving sense of sorrow and even apology. One plinth reads, "Their lives were taken prematurely and wrongly by Mormon militiamen in one of the most tragic episodes in western American history." Another says simply, "They were killed without just cause." There is nothing innovative about these memorials—no architecture magazine would review them. But in a way that is their strength. They acknowledge loss, culpability, and the innocence of the victims.

But what remains absent is a full history of what happened—the deeper history of what lay behind the brutality, and evidence of the ongoing dialogue between descendants and the church. As serene as the site is, it feels almost like a new kind of graveyard—a graveyard of good intentions and failed dialogue.

Manzanar was created not from the top, but from the bottom, by "alumni" of the camp and their children, who began to return for a yearly pilgrimage in 1969. That spirit animates the staff today, who are dedicated to an approach that focuses on storytelling and dialogue. Alisa Lynch, a park ranger who has been at Manzanar for fourteen years, has been the main architect of "humanizing the history" of the site, as she describes it.[16] Under the banner "10,000 people, 10,000 stories" she and her colleagues have chosen to focus less on the national story of racism toward Japanese Americans and more on life in the camp. In the spring of 2015, the staff opened two new barracks, one re-created to show the home life of internees when the camp first opened in

1942, and another to show it toward the end of the war, after they had "settled in" and created their own homes within the prison. Accurate reproductions of cots and tables pale in power, however, to the words and recorded voices of the internees that can be found in the exhibit, collected as part of an ongoing oral history project. The new barracks may be the last building project for the time being. The staff would like to rebuild more of the guard towers since only one remains standing by the road. But the very reason for doing so—to remind visitors that this was a prison camp—is why the neighboring communities are fighting it. The long history of resistance to locating the original camp here in 1942, and then to building the national park site, remains part of the history of the place.

Superintendent Bernadette Johnson explains that the story at Manzanar is one of the "fragility of our rights." At one time or another, "we may all be marginalized."[17] The eighty thousand people who visit Manzanar every year must acknowledge this uneasy lesson. But about three million drive by on highway 395 and perhaps only glance at the mysterious guard tower and the mile of barbed wire they pass on the way to Lake Tahoe.

Shockoe Bottom might be the best place to understand the history of slavery and its ongoing legacy in the United States. If you stand by the remains of Lumpkin's Jail, you can imagine the past experience and present legacy of the buying and selling of African-born people, and their imprisonment in buildings along the creek. You can envision the graves where many of them ended up. Look to the east and you'll see the facades of Tobacco Row, neatly restored buildings rooted in the labor of slaves. Tucked within the Medical Center complex of VCU to the north and west stands the Confederate White House, where Jefferson Davis lived and from which he would have gazed out at Shockoe Bottom, a daily reminder of what the Confederacy was fighting to defend. Looking west across the highway, you can also see a series of skyscrapers, several of them bank buildings, which hold wealth produced by the slave economy. There is a direct line from the commerce in people and the commerce that made—and still makes—white Richmond wealthy, and black Richmond less so. These reasons help explain why, perhaps, earlier Americans considered it important to cover over the place and its memory. The Reverend Monica Esparza, a member of the umbrella group Defenders of Freedom, Justice, and Equality, lamented that she had known nothing of the site, even though her father owned a store in Shockoe Bottom. "Right here in Richmond," she tells me over the rumble of trucks. "I never knew."[18]

The Sacred Ground Reclamation Project was born on October 10, 2004, the 204th anniversary of the execution of Gabriel, a slave who launched an uprising inspired by the Haitian Revolution. It was born in reaction to the plan to build a minor league baseball stadium in Shockoe Bottom, covering up much if not all of what the group considers "sacred ground." That proposal was killed in 2005 but seems to have nine lives; the latest plan is still on the table.[19] Edwards and her allies have had a profound effect on the debate, forcing VCU to give up the parking lot and the city to agree to leave a portion of the land untouched and build a museum around the Lumpkin's Jail site. The computer-generated renderings of the proposed museum are seductive.

But the preservationists aren't satisfied. Like Manzanar, the Sacred Ground Reclamation Project is a member of the International Coalition of Sites of Conscience and advocates dialogue leading to action. For Edwards and the Defenders group, saving and interpreting Shockoe Bottom is not a matter of simply saving a few archaeological remains and putting a roof over them. They are fighting to reclaim the site as part of a larger struggle for a more equal society, which would include economic investment in the black community. They also demand that Americans talk about the need for a larger version of what was won for the victims of Japanese-American internment—monetary reparations. And they insist that Shockoe Bottom cannot be only a story of slavery, or an African American site. As Reverend Esparza says, "This is not an African story—it is the story of all of us."

As self-evident as that statement might seem, the histories of slavery, segregation, and the struggle for—and backlash against—civil rights have just begun to receive the attention they deserve. The story of Shockoe Bottom, of its covering over and more recent honest confrontations with history, is a story that carries resonance throughout the nation.

It may be an odd thing to say about these sites of horrors and atrocities, but I felt uplifted when I visited them. The individual efforts to save and interpret difficult places seem to be part of a larger, potentially powerful movement. I imagine the American body politic—the 320 million people who make up the United States—as a fractured skeleton, bones and vertebrae out of joint, held together and pulled apart at the same time by the actions of people and history. But with the struggles at Manzanar, Mountain Meadows, and Shockoe Bottom, I felt as though I was watching citizen-surgeons in action. With each marking of a horrific event, with each rigorous attempt to uncover the difficult past and present it to the citizens of the present, with each national site that serves as a center of information and dialogue, a part of the nation is put right, realigned, healed.

But like all analogies, mine misses something important. The work is never accomplished once and for all. There is no simple "click," no fix that is complete and permanent. Difficult places are unique because they are first and foremost about the particulars of pain. They are reminders of the specific harm inflicted by one group on another, or the awful conflict between ideals and people. This is the challenge of sites of painful pasts. And it is also the gift they give us. They demand that we interact with their histories, making interpretation and human dialogue central to the experience of a particular place. They make a mockery of the idea that architecture is the only thing that matters in preservation.

This push to preserve and interpret difficult places is changing the preservation movement, not simply because it has demanded that Americans add a new group of sites to the National Register and state and local inventories. The movement demands that Americans rethink the stories they tell at all their historic sites. The movement demands that they "dislodge the curatorial" (in Daniel Bluestone's phrase)[20] and focus on citizens in conversation, in specific places, talking about their shared history.

Mimmo Jodice, *Demetra Opera No. 1*, 1992
(Copyright © Mimmo Jodice, photo courtesy of the artist.)

To confront, of course, does not mean to erase. What countries like Argentina and Germany and now, slowly, the United States have done is make public interpretation at historic sites—monuments, memorials, innovative public art—an ongoing commitment. It is to say, We have to keep talking about our difficult pasts, here, where the past took place, where it was built. We will preserve not to salve wounds, but to pursue a better country.

When I arrived in Rome in January 2014, I saw an image in an exhibition at the American Academy that immediately captured my imagination. It was a photograph by the Italian artist Mimmo Jodice titled *Demetra Opera No. 1* (1992). The photograph shows an ancient bust that lacks much of the right side of its face. But a hand holds in place a reconstruction of the lost piece.

In a way, it is a metaphor for what we traditionally try to do as preservationists—save the object, perhaps restore it, bring it back to life. But I read the image differently. It seems more of a metaphor for our elusive desire to repair a shattered human world. The hand gently holds a repaired piece up to the original, trying to make it fit. But, of course, it does not. Only an approximation of wholeness can be made. And it requires the gentle hand to hold it there, a steady effort.

We cannot erase the injuries of the past. But it seems to me a central duty of historic preservation to lead today's citizens of the world to historic buildings and landscapes that represent humankind's worst histories, or capture our most fundamental disagreements, and, like the hand in Jodice's image, hold us there with creativity and compassion, and make us think again about who we are.

7

beauty

and

justice

In this book, I have argued that preservation should be at the center of several movements for making the world a more just place. Preservation, if broadly understood to be about stewardship of place, can help to save our planet, or at least begin to reverse the damage we have done to it. In the age of voluntary and forced migration, in which nations that may have seen themselves as diverse find they are now far more multicultural than ever before, and countries that saw themselves as relatively homogenous are being forced to confront the diversity within their midst, preservation of controversial places is a crucial tool for achieving reconciliation and consensus. And because it has as a core belief that certain places and values live beyond the market, preservation can be the foundation on which we reassert the idea of the common wealth and in so doing build more just cities.

But where is beauty in this equation? In the effort to move preservation beyond "beautiful architecture" might we lose one of the most important reasons why people want to save, visit, and learn about places? When I go over my notes from travels within the United States and around the world, I am repeatedly confronted with specific instances of beauty in old places. Our lives are marked not only by days and years, births and deaths, graduations and marriages but also by the moments of beauty we have experienced. Each of us has a changing loop of such moments that we can recall with ease. Mine include:

> the sudden, unexpected golden light emanating from buildings on the Campidoglio in Rome after weeks of rain;
>
> a man quietly sweeping the marble plaza of the Taj Mahal at sunrise;
>
> walking up the ramp of the Brooklyn Bridge to the high point over the East River and looking back at the skyline that defines my very idea of "city";
>
> coming across the impossibly complicated look on the face of the Venetian gentleman in Lorenzo Lotto's *Portrait of a Gentleman* (*Ritratto di Gentiluomo*) in the Borghese Gallery in Rome;
>
> standing in the Pantheon, that great gorilla of a building, on Pentecost, when hundreds of red rose petals floated down through the oculus to echoing cheers;

the north rim of the Grand Canyon, at sunset;

swallows swooping around the Hagia Sophia;

the taste of orange juice in the Djemaa el Fna in Marrakesh, as I sit surrounded by the musicians, salesmen, dentists, and magicians of this most electric public square;

walking through Carlo Scarpa's Castelvecchio Museum in Verona, where the artist's distinctive style of intervention, instantly recognizable, somehow manages to be modern and coherent even as it strengthens our appreciation of the medieval castle through the heartbreaking beauty that lies in the care taken with every move, down to the shape of the joints between railings, a visible collaboration between architect and craftsman and an incomparable and improbable merger of individual modernist genius and humble, respectful servant of history.

The beautiful places that make up an important part of our emotional lives come in all forms—paintings, architecture, landscapes, places where uplifting things happened, and even places where horrible things happened. But what unites them is that they all provoke emotions that we often feel lacking in our daily lives. They take us out of ourselves and into the richest feelings we know. In the presence of something we find beautiful, the feeling rushes in before the mind can intellectualize it. "Every now and then," writes Robert Scruton, "we are jolted out of our complacency, and feel ourselves to be in the presence of something vastly more significant than our present interests and desires."[1]

Pentecost Service at the Pantheon, Rome, 2014
At the conclusion of the Mass, thousands of rose petals are dropped through
the oculus onto the congregation.

Castelvecchio Museum, Verona, 2014

The masterpiece of the mid-twentieth-century Italian designer Carlo Scarpa, the Castelvecchio Museum is a powerful blend of modern design and historic preservation that remains a model to this day.

Taj Mahal, Agra, India, 2006
A worker sweeps the plaza beneath the Taj Mahal at dawn.

But the mind plays its part. The beauty jostles us, hits a nerve, the synapses fire, and the mind awakens. The truly beautiful is edifying, in the original meaning of the word: to build up, with instruction and knowledge. We turn the experience over in our minds, seeking sustenance from places and objects, and trying to understand why they provoked tears or awe, and what the experience should teach us. The thinking, the mulling, the turning over the experience in our minds is as essential as that first blush of emotion. The beauty lies in the lasting impact of an experience that might have taken place in a fleeting moment.

The individual emotions tied to the experience of beauty are what make the battles over places important and difficult at the same time. Individuals who find a building or landscape beautiful have an "enduring certitude," in the words of the scholar of aesthetics Elaine Scarry, that the place must be preserved so that everyone, now and in the future, will have the same experience that they did. That is the power of beauty—once convinced that a particular place is beautiful one has a hard time imagining that others might not find that same place beautiful. In some sense what we define as beautiful architecture or a beautiful landscape is nothing more than architecture or a landscape in which generations have found beauty. Individuals and groups, with the tools of law, money, and organization, have convinced society that particular buildings and landscapes are beautiful and that their experience of that beauty matters, to us and to our children and grandchildren.

The changing tides of support for certain buildings—the brownstones of New York City, for example, were despised earlier in the twentieth century but became the centerpieces of gentrification in the final quarter of the century—might suggest that talk of beauty is frivolous, a pandering to shifting tastes. The philosopher Alain de Botton has argued that the reason styles shift over time (often allowing the demolition of once treasured old places) is that we invest in places so much meaning about our own lives. "When we speak of being 'moved' by a building," writes Botton, "we allude to a bitter-sweet feeling of contrast between the noble qualities written into a structure and the sadder wider reality within which we know them to exist." When we say that a building is beautiful, we are implying something "more than a mere aesthetic fondness; [the statement] implies an attraction to the particular way of life this structure is promoting through its roof, door handles, window frames, staircase and furnishings. A feeling of beauty is a sign that we have come upon a material articulation of certain of our ideas of a good life." We preserve historic buildings not simply because we care about how they look, but because overtly or invisibly, we believe they hold within them and their history "the values we want to live by."[2]

Our encounter with beautiful places is marked by the "moment of gasp," as the artist Catie Newell calls it.[3] But in fact, it is the values and meaning—often mysterious and elusive—we attach to places that define the beautiful. Can beauty again be connected to moral fitness, as it was for some in the eighteenth century, or made part of building a better world for all? I am committed to the idea that the beautiful and just are not only related but mutually supportive, necessary and indivisible. The quest to preserve the beautiful and the quest for justice—as problematic as both those concepts are—might have more in common than we usually acknowledge.

My guide in the journey from beauty to justice is Elaine Scarry, whose slim volume *On Beauty and Being Just* recovers beauty from the dustbin of academic critiques and gives it new importance as a means by which we can turn our attention to justice. Scarry bluntly confronts the critiques of beauty, especially in the humanities—its essentialism, the way women are objectified through the term—by refusing to define the word while reaffirming its importance to each person's life. In the pursuit of returning beauty to the center of the humanities, she follows the art critic Dave Hickey, who declared in *The Invisible Dragon* that "beauty is the agency that causes visual pleasure in the beholder, and, since pleasure is the true occasion for looking at anything, any theory of images that is not grounded in the pleasure of the beholder begs the question of art's efficacy and dooms itself to inconsequence!"[4]

Scarry, like Hickey, starts with the "pleasure in the beholder," but wants to argue for the ethical implications of that pleasure. Our experience of beauty, she argues, should lead us in the direction of building a more just world. Beauty "ignites the desire for truth by giving us, with an electric brightness shared by almost no other uninvited, freely arriving perceptual event, the experience of conviction and the experience, as well, of error. . . . It creates, without itself fulfilling, the aspiration for enduring certitude. It comes to us, with no work of our own; then leaves us prepared to undergo a giant labor." Beauty "acquaints us with the mental event of conviction," prompting us "to locate enduring sources of conviction—to locate what is true."[5]

Although I do not believe that scholarship, or music, or art alone can change the world, I do agree with the literary critic George Steiner that "any mature representation of imagined form, any mature endeavor to communicate such representation to another human being, is a moral act." When we are drawn to something and call it "beautiful," this is in part because we recognize the mature, passionate attempt by another person to reveal emotional depths to us. We should not look for "lessons" in art or architecture. But neither should we accept the popular argument that formal expression can or should be divorced from meaning. "The 'purest' work of art," writes Steiner, "the most abstemious from conceivable empirical instruction or appliance, is, by virtue of that very purity and abstention, a sharply political gesture, a value-statement of the most evident ethical import." The "primary texts" of beauty—the work of art, the piece of music, the constructed place—"is a phenomenon of freedom."[6]

Beauty, Scarry argues, encourages replication. When we experience something beautiful we want to share it with someone else. The germ of a democratic sentiment lies in this experience—"You must see this! Everyone should see this!" Beautiful things, she writes, "have a forward momentum"; "they incite the desire to bring new things into the world: infants, epics, sonnets, drawings, dances, laws, philosophic dialogues, theological tracts."[7] Around beautiful objects and places, those from the past and those in the future past, we can build a common bond.

I wish this were so. But our world is filled with great beauty surrounded by great evil, often in close proximity. Many who cherished beauty committed heinous acts, participated in crimes, promoted inequity and racism—sometimes in the midst of the beauty they loved. Hitler, the budding artist who turned to politics, comes to mind. If you visit the Wannsee house in the western suburbs of Berlin where the "final solution" was ratified, you are likely to find the bucolic setting, serene architecture, and lovely art on the walls unsettling. We might wish that the gasp we emit on encountering a beautiful place, a past work of awe-inspiring design, a landscape that evokes unexpected tears would appeal to our best selves. All too often it does not. Beauty, if it propels us toward justice, does so with a faltering engine.

In Lorenzo Lotto's *Annunciation,* one of the thousands of paintings on this central theme of Christianity, Mary is pictured running away from the angel Gabriel. In this, "one of the most un-settling, haunting versions we have of this inexhaustible theme," writes Steiner, Mary "turns her back on the rushing radiance of the Messenger."[8] In the Uffizi Gallery in Florence, in one of the first of the endless rooms filled with one spectacular Italian painting after another, is an Annunciation that I find even more shocking than the one by Lotto. Painted two hundred years earlier, in 1333, the version by Simone Martini and Lippo Memmi presents a scowling Mary giving Gabriel a look of horror. Faced with beauty—and what could be more beautiful than an angelic messenger bring-ing a direct communication from God?—we all also have the freedom to reject or turn away from its message of optimism.

But perhaps we are not looking at beauty in the right way. Scarry precedes her discussion of the way beauty can facilitate justice with a consideration of the "errors" we make in identi-fying beauty, how we sometimes fail to recognize beauty in our midst because our understanding of beauty is too narrow.[9] Yet if we fail to recognize beauty at first, we might learn to do so later. We might start to find beauty in something we once found ugly. And we might find new concepts of beauty, in, for example, the values embodied in otherwise pedestrian forms. Preservation can, if we follow this logic, bring beauty and justice in closer alignment. By preserving the places that embody our highest values, we create an urban fabric of reminders and inspirations whose histories become rallying points for future action. By sav-ing buildings that embody past efforts to achieve a more just society, preservation can offer a powerful continuing argument for those efforts today.

Rosanne Haggerty, a MacArthur Fellow and leader of the organization Community Solutions, got her start fighting for decent housing for the homeless in New York's Times Square. One of her early projects was to renovate the Times Square Hotel. She first made the case that the building had architectural value; this got her the historic preservation tax credits that enabled her to renovate the building for homeless families. A building was saved, people were housed, and architects and artisans found work renovating the building. But for Haggerty, the deeper lesson was "the power of preservation as a worldview and a method for combatting inequality. Preservation's force lay in its unique ability to re-center questions of purpose in planning and development. Dilapidated buildings like the Times Square Hotel seemed of little value, but preservationist thinking urged us to ask, 'Why is this building here in the first place, and what was it originally designed to do?'"[10] By saving a building like the Times Square Hotel, preservationists can solve (or at least ameliorate) an immediate problem. But they can also reintroduce the notion of the public good, a vision of a good society, which has been under attack for a generation in the United States.

Beauty, then, might encompass more than we imagine, and inhere in forms that align with our core values. It might, for example, be found in "ugly" architecture.

My campus, the University of Massachusetts, Amherst, has all too often been summed up with a simple word: *ugly.* At least one online source has awarded it the dubious distinction of being the second ugliest campus in the nation, beaten only by Drexel University in Philadelphia.

In a state filled with manicured campuses featuring picturesque red-brick dormitories and Gothic classrooms, the architecture of our flagship public university is another thing entirely. Colossal concrete slabs, dark subterranean spaces, vertical dormitories—these are the images all too many prospective students conjure up and all too many alumni remember. And the criticisms are not new: in 1974 the *Boston Globe*'s longtime architecture critic, Robert Campbell, called the university "a jumble of unrelated personal monuments that looks more like a world fairgrounds than a campus."[11] As the buildings of the great postwar boom headed toward middle age, there were many who would have been happy for the university to start over, tear down every building on campus, and make way for a completely new look.

The school is a century and a half old, a product of the 1862 Morrill Land Grant Act, but the campus visible today was born after World War II, when the G.I. Bill, which offered virtually free higher education to returning veterans, led the institution to take on bigger ambitions and a new name: the University of Massachusetts. President John Lederle, who led the building boom in the 1960s during its era of greatest growth, saw this expansion as an opportunity to build "a great public center for excellence in higher education": "We have in the University of Massachusetts," he proclaimed, "a potential giant." By 1972, the university had more than twenty-three thousand students, and over 10 million square feet of building space was constructed during the 1960s and 1970s to accommodate them.[12]

This modern public research university was a different institution from the exclusive private colleges for which Massachusetts was known, and its leaders believed that its mission demanded a different look. Instead of mimicking the private schools that had long trained New England elites, the University of Massachusetts (or UMass, as it is affectionately called) would proclaim its distinctive belief in excellence combined with broad educational access for all by embracing the architecture of the day. With plans developed by Sasaki and Associates, and advice on choosing architects from MIT's Pietro Belluschi, President Lederle commissioned the modernist icons that would soon dot the campus: the Southwest Residential Area, designed by Hugh Stubbins; the massive Fine Arts Center complex designed by Kevin Roche and John Dinkeloo; the Lincoln Campus Center, designed by Marcel Breuer; and the McGuirk Alumni Stadium, designed by Skidmore, Owings & Merrill. At the time it was built, in 1973, Edward Durrell Stone's library tower was the tallest building in New England west of Boston and the tallest library in the world. These daring buildings were greeted with enthusiasm, at least in the architectural world. *Architectural Record* devoted a sizable section of its May 1966 issue to a survey of what it headlined "Distinguished Architecture for a State University." The author praised the new buildings as "masterful" and called the UMass approach a model for expanding postwar colleges.[13]

Like many buildings of the period, however, UMass's onetime landmarks have fared poorly over the years. Even as the modernist work of architects like Frank Lloyd Wright, Skidmore, Owings & Merrill, Rudolph Schindler, and Richard Neutra boast ardent partisans, the brutalist concrete monoliths of the 1960s and 1970s have had an especially hard time finding support.

University of Massachusetts, Fine Arts Center, 2006
The Fine Arts Center, with its 646 feet of elevated, north-facing art
studios and 2,000-seat auditorium, was the largest art complex in
New England west of Boston when it was built.

Across the United States, buildings of the period have stood un-
loved or, as often as budgets will allow, been torn down.[14] In
a story familiar to anyone who has spent time in Boston City
Hall, what were initially bright, sculptural forms gave way over
time to stained facades, chipped corners, and broken stairs. The
economic boom of the 1960s and 1970s was followed by two
decades of disinvestment in the university's physical plant, as the
cash-strapped state government scaled down its ambitions. Student growth halted, few new buildings were built, and maintenance of existing structures virtually stopped. Many complaints
about the buildings can be traced to the lack of maintenance

during this period, although real failings in design, construction, and repair coincided with a growing conservative backlash against the New Deal and Great Society. By the end of the 1970s, the buildings that UMass officials had envisioned as marking the start of the university's limitless rise came to be seen by many as hulking monuments to governmental excess and corruption.

As the latest building boom has taken hold, the school's older buildings have drawn the attention of architectural preservationists. A growing number of faculty, staff, and students have come to appreciate the campus as a distinctive entity, not an oppressive one. In 2007, a new organization, Preserve UMass, was founded, with the goal of saving not just the campus's handful of surviving eighteenth- and nineteenth-century buildings but also some of the modern structures that many people find unattractive. Preservation Massachusetts, a statewide nonprofit organization, named the UMass Amherst campus one of the Bay State's "10 Most Endangered Historic Resources." Preservationists have pressured successive campus administrations to deal more thoughtfully with historic buildings and landscapes. The arguments are the ones that have been used by preservationists for decades—these buildings are beautiful in their own right, and they show the continuity of the campus over two centuries.

But these are limited arguments for preserving the campus. Better is this: Built into the UMass campus, and the story of why it looks the way it does, are ideals about what a public university should be. After three decades of a broad national push for smaller federal government and privatized institutions, and in the midst of a statewide debate about taxes, the monumental buildings that helped transform UMass into a major research university remind us who work and study here of different principles: the beliefs that long-term public investment is a value rather than a burden, that working-class as well as wealthy students deserve outstanding learning facilities, that excellent higher education should be affordable to all.

Given the wide differences of public opinion on modern architecture, we can safely assume that the word *ugly* won't be vanishing from conversations about the campus. But it is worth thinking about what it means. The buildings that Americans—as individuals and a society—now think ugly they might later see differently, finding in old architecture new meanings. In the America of today, when the very notion of government having a role in social betterment has been under steady attack, the UMass buildings from America's golden age of public higher education stand for faith in the public sphere. It is possible to look at the library and see only the chips that once fell off some of the bricks, or think about its history of out-of-service elevators. But it is also possible to stand in awe at the idealism of building the world's tallest library, open to everyone twenty-four hours a day. The Fine Arts Center represents a moving decision to commission one of the premier architects of the day to design first-class art, music, and theater spaces for the sons and daughters of the workingmen and women of Massachusetts. Who today would even dare design, as Roche and Dinkeloo did for the Fine Arts Center, a 646-foot-long bridge of studio art space, and raise it up 30 feet from the ground to create a monumental gateway for the campus?

To look at the University of Massachusetts is to see a long debate in brick and steel and concrete about the appropriate image of a major public university. The campus, both its celebrated buildings and its less-beloved ones, is part of a noble story. The UMass buildings have not always been worthy of those dreams. But there are those who believe that in deciding how to equip the university for the next century, we should not see the heroic buildings of the 1960s and 1970s as the enemy. Rather, they are landmarks, pointing to what must always be the founding ideals of our flagship campus: public investment in our public schools and a belief that precisely this kind of institution is the cornerstone of democracy.

Ugliness at the University of Massachusetts, and in public universities across the country, becomes beauty of purpose when looked at the right way. Other places can embody beauty in different ways. And places that are widely regarded as beautiful by architectural standards might, through the impact of events, acquire a new beauty.

After the attacks on September 11, 2001, the *New York Times* architectural critic Herbert Muschamp suggested that as the city and nation debated the future of "Ground Zero" and the city more generally, people should take time to think about their favorite places in New York.[15] For me, that was easy: the New York Public Library.

It is not far from the truth to say that I chose the topic of my first book for the opportunity to study in the New York Public Library's main reading room. The thought that the next Alfred Kazin or Betty Friedan might be sitting next to me—perhaps in

New York Public Library Reading Room, 2003
There are few places as inspiring as this room, a full block long, sumptuously furnished and ornamented, and open to everyone seeking a book, a place to study, a table to write at, a space to be inspired by.

the guise of a muttering, smelly citizen or a studious immigrant—was inspirational. If the reading room is the grandest of public places, it is also the most sublime of private places: an ennobling hall of peopled solitude. Nestled into a great oak chair, with a lamp shining a circle over a book, a reader can feel truly, and often frighteningly, alone. But the diverse sounds of the intellectual jungle fill the room: book carts squealing on their reshelving journeys, shoes clicking as patrons make their walk up the aisle to retrieve their books, expectorations of annoyance at a lost book or a disappearing thought, the swoosh of turning pages, the hiss of gossiping students, and the almost audible sound of people reading and thinking.

In a city of intense human and architectural congestion, one comes to crave the long view, the experience of vast space. New York's greatest designer, Frederick Law Olmsted, built parks that offered the gift of distance to those whose longest domestic vista came from peering across a tenement's airshaft. If anything is to be cherished in New York, it is the expenditure of space for people and lives led in public. Looking across the reading room, from one end to the other, still gives me the same exhilarating feel as walking in Prospect Park in Brooklyn, Olmsted's masterpiece, strolling gently down winding paths dense with trees, and then, suddenly, emerging into a mile-long view of the Long Meadow. As Tom Stoppard wrote in *The Invention of Love,* "We catch our breath at the places where the breath was always caught"[16]—at an unexpected gift of beauty. The New York Public Library reading room, offering a block-long view of diverse patrons engaged in a common project of contemplation alongside hundreds of other New Yorkers, is a gift that always lifts the soul.

If any profession naively seeks immortality in the tangible world, it is architecture. Architects aspire to build "timeless" buildings that will stand and be revered for the ages. Carrere and Hastings, the architects of the 42nd Street library, built a beautiful building and cloaked it in the ever-popular Classical Revival style in order to give it the best chance for eternal life. The library will come as close as any to achieving that impossible dream, but perhaps less for the artistic beauty it offers New Yorkers than for the cultural meaning that it holds within it. If cities remain the places where diverse races, ethnicities, and classes, but also ideas and politics, mix, mingle and often clash, it is on the public stages of the city that this central drama will be played out. The social health of all the world's cities—not just their visual appeal—requires not only that we build but that we preserve these places. If the preservation movement dedicates itself to economic justice and not just economic development, it will do more than save beautiful buildings; it will be a preserver of our built ideals.

CHAPTER ONE: NOT YOUR GRANDMOTHER'S
PRESERVATION MOVEMENT

1. In this chapter I draw from my article "Values Added: It's Not Your Grandmother's Preservation Society," *ArchitectureBoston* 18, no. 3, issue titled *Preserve* (Fall 2015): 32–35.

2. Paul Goldberger, *Why Architecture Matters* (New Haven: Yale University Press, 2011), 200.

3. Tony Kushner, *Slavs!,* in Kushner, *Thinking About Longstanding Problems of Virtue and Happiness* (New York: Theater Communications Group, 1995), 108.

4. Tom Mayes's series of blog posts, "Why Do Old Places Matter?," is at the Preservation Leadership Forum blog, http://blog.preservation leadershipforum.org/why-do-old-places-matter/#.VmWbAuMrKBY. I discuss them in Chapter 2.

CHAPTER TWO: WHY WE PRESERVE

1. The opening page of this chapter is adapted from my essay "Madeleine Moments: All We Know of Heaven," *ArchitectureBoston* 15, no. 3, issue titled *Memory* (Fall 2012): 22.

2. Maurice Halbwachs, *On Collective Memory* (Chicago: University of Chicago Press, 1992), 122.

3. Joseph Schumpeter, *Capitalism, Socialism, and Democracy* (New York: Harper and Row, 1942).

4. The National Historic Preservation Act (October 15, 1966), as Amended Through December 19, 2014, and Codified in Title 54 of the United States Code, http://www.achp.gov/docs/NHPA%20in%20 Title%2054%20and%20Conversion%20Table.pdf.

5. Tom Mayes, "Why Do Old Places Matter?" the Preservation Leadership Forum blog, http://blog.preservationleadershipforum.org/why -do-old-places-matter/#.VmWbAuMrKBY (viewed October 4, 2015).

6. Ibid.

7. Mumford, quoted in Nathan Silver, *Lost New York* (Boston: Houghton Mifflin, 1967), 9.

8. Wim Wenders's exhibition *Urban Solitude* was on display from April 18 to July 6, 2014 at the Palazzo Incontro in Rome.

9. The transformation of the meaning of the Lincoln Memorial is discussed in Scott A. Sandage, "A Marble House Divided: The Lincoln Memorial, the Civil Rights Movement, and the Politics of Memory, 1939–1963," *Journal of American History* 80, no. 1 (June 1993): 135–67. See also Christopher A. Thomas, *The Lincoln Memorial and American Life* (Princeton: Princeton University Press, 2002), and Tom Mayes, "Why Old Places Matter," the section "Memory."

10. Gaston Bachelard, *Poetics of Space* (Boston: Beacon, 1994), 6.

11. Rodney Harrison, *Heritage: Critical Approaches* (New York: Routledge, 2012), 3.

12. Pierre Nora, "Between Memory and History," *Representations* 26, Special issue, *Memory and Counter-Memory* (Spring, 1989): 7–24; Yosef Hayim Yerushalmi, *Zakhor: Jewish History and Jewish Memory* (1983; New York: Schocken, 1989), xxvii.

13. Rosenzweig, quoted in Yerushalmi, *Zakhor,* 98.

14. Karsten Harries, "The Ethical Function of Architecture," *Journal of Architectural Education* 29, no. 1 (1975): 14.

15. Nora, "Between Memory and History," 9.

16. Rem Koolhaas, "Preservation Is Overtaking Us," *Future Anterior* 1, no. 2 (Fall 2004): 1.

17. Martin Heidegger, "Building Dwelling Thinking," in his *Poetry, Language, Thought* (1971; New York: Harper Perennial, 2013), 159.

18. Yerushalmi, *Zakhor,* 97.

19. Richard Todd, *The Thing Itself: On the Search for Authenticity* (New York: Riverhead, 2008).

20. Lionel Trilling, *Sincerity and Authenticity* (Cambridge: Harvard University Press, 1972), 6, 10n1, 118–19.

21. See John Ruskin, "The Lamp of Memory," in his *Seven Lamps of Architecture* (1849; New York: Dover, 1989), 163–82.

22. Marinetti, quoted in Trilling, *Sincerity and Authenticity,* 129.

23. Trilling, *Sincerity and Authenticity,* 101, 131; Heidegger, "Building Dwelling Thinking," 141–42.

24. Walter Benjamin, "The Work of Art in the Age of Mechanical Reproduction," in Benjamin, *Illuminations: Essays and Reflections,* trans. Harry Zohn (New York: Schocken, 1969).

25. Thornton Wilder, *Our Town* (New York: Harper, 2003), 4.

CHAPTER THREE: HOW AMERICANS PRESERVE

1. The process for registration with the National Register is laid out in detail in the National Register bulletin *How to Complete the National Registration Form,* available at http://www.nps.gov/nr/publications/bulletins/pdfs/nrb16a.pdf.

2. See Max Page and Steve Balkin, "Chicago's Preservation Blues," *Christian Science Monitor,* December 28, 2000.

3. See Max Page and Randall Mason, eds., *Giving Preservation a History: Histories of Historic Preservation in the United States* (New York: Routledge, 2003).

4. Ned Kaufman, *Place, Race, and Story: Essays on the Past and Future of Historic Preservation* (New York: Routledge, 2009), 297.

5. This discussion draws from "The Gerrymandered Lower East Side Historical District," *New York Daily News,* April 26, 2001.

6. Ernest Becker, *The Denial of Death* (New York: Free Press, 1973).

7. Adrienne LaFrance, "At Least 1,750 Sites Removed from the National Register of Historic Places Since 1970," *Ukiah Daily Journal,* February 10, 2013, at http://www.ukiahdailyjournal.com/20130210/at -least-1750-sites-removed-from-the-national-register-of-historic-places -since-1970. A single listing may include a historic district with dozens or even hundreds of historic "resources." There are about 90,540 "listings" comprising 1,752,995 total contributing resources (including buildings, sites, structures, objects, etc.). In 2014, 1,030 properties were added to the list. See the National Register of Historic Places, National Park Service website, http://www.nps.gov/nr/index.htm, for November 29, 2015.

8. Rodney Harrison, *Heritage: Critical Approaches* (New York: Routledge, 2012), 197. Rem Koolhaas has suggested that rather than continually expanding lists of historic places, Americans should preserve a whole swath of a city—miles long and hundreds of feet wide—for a period of time, and then allow it to be redeveloped while another area is set aside. This is actually anti-management. While it has the provocative virtue of challenging preservationists to save the evidence of an entire era, it also denies the democratic possibility of debating what we should care to save or allow to disappear. See Rem Koolhaas, *Preservation Is Overtaking Us* (New York: Graduate School of Architecture, Planning and Preservation, Columbia University, 2014).

9. Sharon MacDonald, *Difficult Heritage: Negotiating the Past in Nuremberg and Beyond* (New York: Routledge, 2008). See also Alison Smale, "Nuremberg Nazi Site Crumbles, but Tricky Questions on Its Future Persist," *New York Times,* November 2, 2015.

10. See, for example, the plea by then-president of the Metropolitan Museum of Art, Philippe Montebello, to save the ruin of one of the towers. "The Iconic Power of the Artifact," *New York Times* 25 September 2001.

11. James Marston Fitch, *Curatorial Management of the Built Environment* (Charlottesville: University of Virginia Press, 1990).

12. Anthony Doerr, *Four Seasons in Rome* (New York: Scribner's, 2007), 40.

13. Marc Bloch, *Idol of Origins* (New York: Knopf, 1953), 29.

14. Patricia Parker and Thomas F. King, *Guidelines for Evaluating and Documenting Traditional Cultural Properties,* National Park Service, Bulletin 38, 1998.

15. Bohemian Hall and Park, Place Matters, http://placematters.net/node/1044 (accessed November 23, 2015).

CHAPTER FOUR: PRESERVATION AND ECONOMIC JUSTICE

1. For similar comments see, e.g., the report written by Donovan D. Rypkema and Caroline Cheong, *Measuring the Economics of Preservation: Recent Findings,* prepared for the Advisory Council on Historic Preservation by PlaceEconomics, June 2011, http://www.achp.gov/docs/final-popular-report6-7-11.pdf.

2. A number of these studies have been synthesized ibid. and in a report of the Brookings Institution by Randall Mason, *Economics and Historic Preservation: A Guide and Review of the Literature* (September 2005), at http://www.brookings.edu/research/reports/2005/09/metropolitanpolicy-mason.

3. I heard these complaints at a meeting of preservationists sponsored by the National Trust, the University of Massachusetts, and the University of Pennsylvania at Kykuit, the Rockefeller estate on the Hudson, May 27–29, 2015.

4. Edward Glaeser, *Triumph of the City: How Our Greatest Invention Makes Us Richer, Smarter, Greener, Healthier, and Happier* (New York: Penguin, 2011); Edward Glaeser, "Preservation Follies," *City Journal* 20, no. 2 (Spring 2010).

5. Erin Carlyle, "Manhattan's New Most Expensive Listing: A $130 Million Park Avenue Penthouse," *Forbes,* September 24, 2014; Adam Gopnik, "Naked Cities," *New Yorker,* October 5, 2015, 85.

6. Andrew Hurley, "Making Preservation Work for Struggling Communities: A Plea to Loosen National Historic District Guidelines," in *Bending the Future: Fifty Ideas for the Next Fifty Years of Historic Preservation,* ed. Max Page and Marla R. Miller (Amherst: University of Massachusetts Press, 2016), 117.

7. Preservation Green Lab, *Older, Smaller, Better: Measuring How the Character of Buildings and Blocks Influences Urban Vitality* (Washington, D.C.: National Trust for Historic Preservation, 2014), 1.

8. Michael Sorkin, "Preserving People," in *Bending the Future,* 226. In one unusual name change, the block where Spike Lee's *Do the Right Thing* was filmed was recently renamed Do the Right Thing Way. See http://www.bizjournals.com/newyork/news/2015/07/24/bed-stuy-re named-for-do-the-right-thing-spike-lee.html.

9. Suleiman Osman, "Preserving the History of Gentrification," in *Bending the Future,* 191.

10. See Japonica Brown-Saracino, *A Neighborhood That Never Changes: Gentrification, Preservation, and the Search for Authenticity* (Chicago: University of Chicago Press, 2010).

11. Freeman, quoted in Adam Sternbergh, "What's Wrong with Gentrification? The Displacement Myth, *New York,* December 11, 2009, available at: http://nymag.com/news/intelligencer/62675/.

12. Ibid.; Andrew Hurley, *Beyond Preservation: Using History to Revitalize Inner Cities* (Philadelphia: Temple University Press, 2010); Brad White comment at preservation meeting at Kykuit, the Rockefeller estate on the Hudson, May 27–29, 2015; Sternbergh, "What's Wrong with Gentrification?"

13. The debate over modifying zoning to encourage more private-market development in Harlem has roiled the community. See the editorial "Affordable Housing vs. Gentrification," *New York Times,* November 27, 2015. At the same time, following examples from other cities, New York's de Blasio and the City Council have recently shifted the emphasis toward affordable housing, in part by requiring developers to include affordable housing units, including for those below the median income. See J. David Goodman, "New York Passes Rent Rules to Blunt Gentrification," *New York Times,* March 22, 2016.

14. Hurley, "Making Preservation Work for Struggling Communities," 30.

15. Sorkin, "Preserving People," 223, 224.

16. Information on Project Row Houses and Rebuild Foundation can be found at the organizations' respective websites, http://project rowhouses.org/ and https://rebuild-foundation.org.

17. For City Life see Catherine Elton, "Foreclose This!" *Boston Magazine* (November 2011), http://www.bostonmagazine.com/2011/11/fore close-this-boston-homeowners-fight-back/, and Akilah Johnson, "Mel King, 2 Other Activists Arrested During Eviction Protest, *Boston Globe,* October 4, 2013, available at https://www.bostonglobe.com/metro/2013/ 10/03/mel-king-other-activists-arrested-during-eviction-protest/L9a prZqXoK1bMLYfLs6ZiM/story.html; Graciela Isabel Sánchez, "Preservationists Must Be Anti-Gentrification Activists," in *Bending the Future,* 214: "In San Antonio, the struggle to prevent gentrification is going to have to take on some of the most formidable economic interests in the City because inner-city redevelopment promises huge profits and historic preservation is at risk of becoming mere 'value added' for the developers" (216).

18. Paul Krugman, "Why Not a WPA?" *New York Times* November 6, 2009; The Daily Team, the Thom Hartman Program, "Time for a New Works Progress Administration?" *Truthout,* January 16, 2014, http://www .truth-out.org/opinion/item/21282-time-for-a-new-works-progress-admin istration; Amber Wiley, "A Modern-Day WPA," in *Bending the Future,* 261.

1. See the Holyoke Gas and Electric Company statistics at its website: http://www.hged.com/community-environment/green%20initiative/hydro/default.aspx and http://hged.com/about/history/default.aspx (accessed October 15, 2015).

2. The Political Research Institute at the University of Massachusetts has charted the economic benefits of a "green economy." See *Job Opportunities for the Green Economy: A State-by-State Picture of Occupations that Gain from Green Investments,* last updated March 7, 2016, at http://www.peri.umass.edu/green_jobs/. See also Robert Pollin, Heidi Garrett-Peltier, James Heintz, and Bracken Hendricks, *Green Growth: A U.S. Program for Controlling Climate Change and Expanding Job Opportunities,* September 18, 2014, Center for American Progress, https://www.americanprogress.org/issues/green/report/2014/09/18/96404/green-growth/.

3. Daniel Bluestone, "Architecture's Stepchild?" *ArchitectureBoston* 18, no. 3, issue titled *Preserve* (Fall 2015): 27.

4. National Historic Preservation Act (Public Law No. 89-665, as amended by Pub. L. No. 96-515), section 1, available at http://www.achp.gov/docs/NHPA%20in%20Title%2054%20and%20Conversion%20Table.pdf.

5. Mike Jackson has summarized and updated this research neatly in "Embodied Energy and Historic Preservation: A Needed Reassessment," *Association for Preservation Technology Bulletin* 36, no. 4 (2005): 47–52. See also Jean Carroon's comprehensive look at the state of the field, *Sustainable Preservation: Greening Existing Buildings* (Hoboken, N.J.: Wiley, 2010).

6. Preservation Green Lab, *The Greenest Building: Quantifying the Environmental Value of Building Reuse* (National Trust for Historic Preservation, 2011), at http://www.preservationnation.org/information-center/sustainable-communities/green-lab/lca/The_Greenest_Building_low

res.pdf. See also Jean Carroon, "Old Is the New Green," *Architecture-Boston* 18, no. 3, issue titled *Preserve* (Fall 2015): 36–39, at http://www.archi tects.org/architectureboston/articles/old-new-green.

7. Jennifer O'Connor, "Survey on Actual Service Lives for North American Buildings," paper presented at Woodframe Housing Durability and Disaster Issues conference, Las Vegas, October 2004, http://www.woodworks.org/wp-content/uploads/2012/02/fpi-survey-actual-service-lives.pdf.

8. Richard Moe and Carter Wilkie, *Changing Places: Rebuilding Community in the Age of Sprawl* (New York: Henry Holt, 1997). See also Moe, "This Old Wasteful House," *New York Times,* April 6, 2009.

9. Jane Jacobs, *The Death and Life of Great American Cities* (New York: Modern Library, 1961), 187.

10. Ibid.

11. David Owen, *Green Metropolis: Why Living Smaller, Living Closer, and Driving Less Are the Keys to Sustainability* (New York: Riverhead, 2010). It is important to note, however, that people living in rural Africa will for the foreseeable future have a far smaller carbon footprint than those living in "green" American cities. The number of things they purchase and consume and the amount they travel alone makes even New Yorkers some of the least "green" people on earth.

12. Jacobs, *Death and Life of Great American Cities,* 54. Jacobs writes, "We are the lucky possessors of a city order that makes it relatively simple to keep the peace because there are plenty of eyes on the street."

13. Ibid., 448.

14. See the LEED calculator at the U.S. Green Building Council webpage, http://www.usgbc.org/credits/neighborhood-development-plan/v4/green-infrastructure-%26-buildings.

15. See "Historic Preservation and Adaptive Reuse," *LEED ND: Built Project |v4 - LEED v4,* at http://www.usgbc.org/node/2613697?return=/credits.

16. Stephen Mouzon, "Is It Time for the Anti-LEED?" *Arch Daily,*

October 15, 2014, at http://www.archdaily.com/557605/is-it-time-for
-the-anti-leed; See also Barbara A. Campagna, "How Changes to LEED™
Will Benefit Existing and Historic Buildings," the American Institute
of Architects website, http://www.aia.org/practicing/groups/kc/AIAS
076321.

17. See the Living Building Challenge website at http://living-future.
org/lbc .

18. Preservation Green Lab, *Saving Windows, Saving Money: Evaluating the Energy Performance of Window Retrofit and Replacement*
(National Trust for Historic Preservation, 2012), at http://www.preser
vationnation.org/information-center/sustainable-communities/green-lab/
saving-windows-saving-money/.

19. Moe, "This Old Wasteful House."

20. Bluestone, "Architecture's Stepchild?"

21. Tom Mayes, "Changing the Paradigm from Demolition to
Reuse—Building Reuse Ordinances," in *Bending the Future: Fifty Ideas
for the Next Fifty Years of Historic Preservation,* ed. Max Page and Marla
R. Miller (Amherst: University of Massachusetts Press, 2016), 162–65.

22. Michael Braungart and William McDonough, *Cradle to Cradle:
Remaking the Way We Make Things* (New York: North Point, 2002).

23. Tracie Rozhon, "Old Baltimore Row Houses Fall Before Wrecking Ball," *New York Times,* June 13, 1999. Many planners and policy
experts argued that the difficulty of maintaining and rebuilding abandoned row houses made the demolition strategy a logical one. See Allan
Mallach, *Laying the Groundwork for Change: Demolition, Urban Strategy, and Policy Reform* (Washington, D.C.: Brookings Metropolitan
Policy Program, 2012). Maryland will spend $700 million more to
demolish those four thousand vacant homes. See Luke Broadwater
and Yvonne Wenger, "Gov. Hogan Announces $700M Plan to Target
Urban Decay in Baltimore," *Baltimore Sun,* January 5, 2016.

24. Jacobs, *Death and Life of Great American Cities,* p. 204.

25. Nicholas Kulish, "German City Wonders How Green Is Too

Green," *New York Times,* August 6, 2008; Thomas Friedman, "Germany, the Green Superpower," *New York Times,* May 6, 2015; Herman K. Trabish, "Lancaster, CA Becomes First U.S. City to Require Solar," March 27, 2013, *Greentech Media,* at http://www.greentechmedia.com/articles/read/Lancaster-CA-Becomes-First-US-City-to-Require-Solar.

26. Steve Mouzon, "Preservation vs. LEED," May 6, 2009, *Original Green,* http://www.originalgreen.org/blog/preservation-vs-leed.html. See Stephen A. Mouzon, *The Original Green: Unlocking the Mystery of True Sustainability* (Miami: The New Urban Guild Foundation, 2010).

27. See David Glassberg, Max Page, and Nicholas Bromell, "Conserving the Commons: Democracy, Ecology and the Places that Matter," NEH grant proposal, June 2015, in possession of the author.

28. Tony Hiss, "A Grand Coalition," in *Bending the Future,* 113.

CHAPTER SIX: PRESERVING AND
INTERPRETING DIFFICULT PLACES

1. Naomi Klein, *The Shock Doctrine: The Rise of Disaster Capitalism* (New York: Metropolitan Books, 2007), 589, 585–86. This chapter is adapted from two articles, "Why We Need Bad Places," *Forum Journal* 29, no. 3, special issue, *Why Do Old Places Matter?* (Spring 2015), and "Sites of Conscience: Shockoe Bottom, Manzanar, and Mountain Meadows," *Preservation Magazine,* Fall 2015.

2. Avishai Margalit, *The Ethics of Memory* (Cambridge: Harvard University Press, 2002), 5.

3. Ned Kaufman, *Place, Race and Story* (New York: Routledge, 2009), 401.

4. Max Page, "Sites of Conscience: Shockoe Bottom, Manzanar, and Mountain Meadows," *Preservation Magazine* (Fall 2015).

5. One of the best books on Mussolini's relationship to and transformation of Rome is Joshua Arthurs, *Excavating Modernity: The Roman Past in Fascist Italy* (Ithaca: Cornell University Press, 2012). Arthurs's

discussion of the debate over tearing down or altering the Foro Italico in preparation for the 1960 Olympics became relevant in the debate in 2015 over renaming the Woodrow Wilson School of Public and International Affairs at Princeton University because of Wilson's racist views and policies, and renaming Calhoun College at Yale because of John Calhoun's central role in articulating the defense of slavery before the Civil War. See Joshua Rothman, "Names in the Ivy League," *New Yorker,* November 26, 2015.

6. Max Page, "The Roman Architecture of Mussolini, Still Standing," *Boston Globe,* July 13, 2014.

7. Ibid.

8. Robert Musil, "Monuments," in Musil, *Posthumous Papers of a Living Author,* trans. Peter Wortsman (Hygiene, Colo.: Eridanos, 1987).

9. The writing about Berlin's memorial landscape is extensive. The best starting points are James Young, *The Texture of Memory: Holocaust Memorials and Meaning* (New Haven: Yale University Press, 1993); Brian Ladd, *The Ghosts of Berlin: Confronting German History in the Urban Landscape* (Chicago: University of Chicago Press, 1998); and Michael Z. Wise, *Capital Dilemma: German's Search for a New Architecture of Democracy* (Princeton: Princeton Architectural Press, 1998).

10. The finest book on this period is Marguerite Feitlowitz, *A Lexicon of Terror: Argentina and the Legacies of Torture* (1998; New York: Oxford University Press, 2012).

11. Ibid., 4.

12. Memoria Abierta, *Memories in the City: Signs of State Terrorism in Buenos Aires,* ed. Max Page (Amherst: University of Massachusetts Press, 2014).

13. Page, "Sites of Conscience."

14. The best history of Japanese internment is Richard Reeves, *Infamy: The Shocking Story of the Japanese American Internment in World War II* (New York: Holt, 2012).

15. See Sally Denton, *American Massacre: The Tragedy at Mountain Meadows, September 1857* (New York: Knopf, 2003).

16. Page, "Sites of Conscience."

17. Ibid.

18. Ibid.

19. The National Trust for Historic Preservation has dedicated an enormous amount of energy to advocating for appropriate preservation and interpretation of the site; see the information about Shockoe Bottom at the National Trust web site: https://savingplaces.org/places/shockoe-bottom#.Vv2B5k32aUl.

20. Daniel Bluestone, "Dislodging the Curatorial," in *Bending the Future: Fifty Ideas for the Next Fifty Years of Historic Preservation,* ed. Max Page and Marla R. Miller (Amherst: University of Massachusetts Press, 2016), 53.

CHAPTER SEVEN: BEAUTY AND JUSTICE

1. Robert Scruton, *Beauty: A Very Short Introduction* (New York: Oxford University Press, 2011).

2. Alain de Botton, *The Architecture of Happiness* (New York: Pantheon, 2006), 22, 72, 73.

3. Quoted in Tom Mayes, "Why Do Old Places Matter?" the Preservation Leadership Forum blog, http://blog.preservationleadershipforum.org/2014/02/07/old-places-matter-beauty/.

4. Elaine Scarry, *On Beauty and Being Just* (Princeton: Princeton University Press, 1999); Dave Hickey, *The Invisible Dragon: Essays on Beauty* (1993; Chicago: University of Chicago Press, 2012),2.

5. Scarry, *On Beauty and Being Just,* 53, 31.

6. George Steiner, *Real Presences* (Chicago: University of Chicago Press, 1990),143, 144–45, 151.

7. Scarry, *On Beauty and Being Just,* 47.

8. Steiner, *Real Presences,* 146.

9. Scarry, *On Beauty and Being Just,* 48.

10. Rosanne Haggerty, "Keeping Us Honest: What Our Buildings Tell Us About the Health of Our Communities," in *Bending the Future: Fifty Ideas for the Next Fifty Years of Historic Preservation,* ed. Max Page and Marla R. Miller (Amherst: University of Massachusetts Press, 2016).

11. Robert Campbell, "A Prototype, but Never to Be Repeated," *Boston Globe,* January 6, 1974.

12. See Marla R. Miller and Max Page, *The University of Massachusetts Amherst Campus Guide* (Princeton: Princeton Architectural Press, 2013), 27.

13. Mildred Schmertz, "Distinguished Architecture for a State University," *Architectural Record* (May 1966), 170–79.

14. For a discussion of the preservation of modernism see Theodore Prudon, *Preservation of Modern Architecture* (New York: Wiley, 2008), as well as the website of the International Committee for the Documentation and Conservation of Buildings, Sites, and Neighborhoods of the Modern Movement, better known as DOCOMOMO—docomomo -us.org. The best book on a key architect of this period, Paul Rudolph, is Timothy M. Rohan, *The Architecture of Paul Rudolph* (New Haven: Yale University Press, 2014).

15. Herbert Muschamp, "For Rebuilders, Inspiration All Around," *New York Times,* October 5, 2001.

16. Tom Stoppard, *The Invention of Love* (London: Grove, 1998), 35.

index

Page numbers in *italics* indicate illustrations.

nostalgia, 33
Nuremberg, Germany, 61

Obama, Barack, 89, 97
Olmsted, Frederick Law, 182
Operation Condor, 144
Orchard Street, New York, 79
Osman, Suleiman, 88
Owen, David, 113
ownership: forms of property, 93–94;
    land trusts, 8, 94

Pain Quotidien, 75, 78
Paiute Indians, 153
Palatine Hill, Rome, 134
Pantheon, Rome, 134, 164, *166*
Paris, France, 4
Park Avenue Armory, New York, 63
Parque de la Memoria, Buenos Aires,
    146
PassivHaus, 118, 122
Pennsylvania Station, New York, 5,
    6, 12
Philadelphia, Pennsylvania, 74
Pike Place Market, Seattle, 10
Pilsen, Chicago, 91
Place Matters, 127
"places that matter," 127
Portelli, Alessandro, 138
Preservation Massachusetts, 178
Preserve UMass, 178
Presidio, San Francisco, 10
Project Row Houses, Houston, 94
Prospect Park, Brooklyn, New York,
    182

Quincy Market, Boston, 10

RCA, 71
real estate market, 12, 54, 70, 77, 79
Reichstag, Berlin, 142
renewable energy and preservation,
    124
rent regulations, 94
Revolutionary Armed Forces of
    Colombia (FARC), 1
Richardson, Henry Hobson, 19, 104
Richmond, Virginia, 12, 17, 70, 149
Robinson, Jimmie Lee, 47, 51; "Max-
    well Street Teardown Blues," 48, 51
Roche, Kevin, 124, 176
Rockefeller, John D., 132; Kykuit,
    New York, 132
Roma and Sinti, memorial to,
    142–43
Roman Forum, 26, 64
Rome, Italy, 26, 33, 63–65, 137, 160.
    *See also individual streets and
    landmarks*
Rosenzweig, Franz, 31
Rossi, Aldo, 97
ruins, 33
Ruskin, John, 36–37
Rypkema, Donovan, 69

Sacred Ground Historical Reclama-
    tion Project, 70, 132, 151, 157
Saint Mary's Church, New York, 57
Saint Peter's Square, Rome, 134
Sánchez, Graciela Isabel, 95
San Francisco, California, 10, 18
Savannah, Georgia, 62
Scarpa, Carlo, Castelvecchio
    Museum, Verona, 165, *167*
Scarry, Elaine, 170–71, 173

Max Page is professor of architecture and history at the University of Massachusetts, Amherst. He is the author of *The Creative Destruction of Manhattan, 1900–1940* and *The City's End: Two Centuries of Fantasies, Fears, and Premonitions of New York's Destruction*. Page is a winner of the Spiro Kristof Award from the Society of Architectural Historians as well as a Guggenheim Fellowship, and a Rome Prize from the American Academy in Rome.